SUPERHUMAN YOU ARE

LIVE RICH AND HEALTHY LIFE

KHAN JAHANGIR KHAN

ISBN
Hardcase 979-8-89744-689-6
Paperback 979-8-89632-767-7

Dedicated to

My dear friend

SUPERHUMAN SONU SOOD

"A book is equal to a friend & a good friend is equal to a library."

– APJ Abdul Kalam

Contents

PART - 2

Introduction of the Author

Born in Delhi, Khan Jahangir Khan (Django),did his education from Delhi only. In 1984 - 85 completed an acting Course from Sri Ram center for art and culture.Then joined a repertory company as a professional actor and acted in more than 30 plays. Moved to Mumbai in 1989 for working in Bollywood and acted in his first movie Aashiqui directed by Mahesh Bhatt. He has worked with Bollywood personalities such as:

Prakash Jha, Tigmanshu Dhulia, Mahesh Bhatt, Sunil Bohra, Anubhav Sinha, Nana Patekar, Amitabh Bachchan, Shahrukh Khan, Salman Khan, Akshay Kumar, Katrina Kaif, Ramgopal Verma, Anurag Kashyap, Irrfan Khan, Anil Senior, Dharmendra, Bobby Deol, Nawazuddin Siddiqui, Manoj Vajpayee, Anubhav Sinha, Rimi Sen, Ajay Devgn, Kajol, Bipasha Basu, Mahi. Gill, Alia Bhatt, Sanjay Dutt, Puja Bhatt, K.K Menon, Jimmy Shergill, Anupam Kher, Rajpal Yadav, Rajkumar Santoshi, Sonakshi Sinha, Varun Dhawan, Naseeruddin Shah, Shabana Azmi, Tabu, Jackline Farnandis, Sanjay Leela Bhansali, Jaideep Ahlawat, Shefali Shah, Vipul Shah, Sunny Deol & Nitesh Tiwari.

T.V. & Web series:

Trikaal, Parivartan, Ummeed, Kasak, Mohalla Mohabbat Wala, Amma, Inspector Avinash, Ashram, Udhamgadh & many more.

Hindi feature films:

Aashiqui, Sadak, Prahaar, Charas, Pehla Nasha, Shagird, Escape from taliban, Staying alive, hafta bandh, Apaharan, Raajneeti, Ab Tak chhappan 2, Raajneeti, Dilwale, Sankat city, Paan Singh Tomar, Raag Desh,Gauru, Gangubai, Bhola, Fateh,Bole chudiyan, Hisaab & Ramayana.

Preface

Salute to each of you individual superhuman, Who are reading this book. I am grateful to The Creator who has bestowed the superhuman idea on me! By applying the superhuman formula, I have practically managed to get rid of maximum problems & diseases of mine like low BP, arthritis, slip disc, sickness, varicose veins, sinus, acidity, depression & a big cyst on my left kidney & that is without taking any medicine. I have disposed of all the useless anger & arrogance too! You can also heal yourself as you have the power to heal.

All the certified superhumans of the world have shown us the power of the human mind and body, time & again. They all conduct their teaching classes to enhance other human's machine. They all say you can do it, too because all humans of the world have the same software (mind) and hardware(body). Which proves that we are all born superhumans. By understanding and applying the superhuman formula, your life will be more exciting and less painful. Some of you already know and enjoy a superhuman life. They are using their superpowers. Buying an island and a private jet is very easy for them and a few of them could walk on the moon, too but many of us are repenting for even being born. Because most of us don't know how to use our superpowers more & more. I am absolutely sure after complete reading this book you will understand it easily. Whenever we plan for something big, we need to understand the concept/subject in detail, so why not know more about our own mind and body very well?

What is the purpose of this book?

A 'Healthy-wealthy life' is a human's first priority! We humans need to understand our mind & body mechanisms Scientifically, and only then can we enjoy our superpowers to make our lives healthy-wealthy! Many of you are already living much healthier & wealthier than me, so it means you are living superhuman life to the next level which I am eager to live. So how come this book going to help you?

Every person is eager to achieve their next level in every field of life, so this book surely will take you to your next level. All human lives are similar to each other but are very different in many ways. For example:

Where are we born? Who are our parents?

What has our atmosphere been from the beginning to date? Who are our friends and relatives?

What are Are we doing or used to do? Are we rich or poor... etcetera...? There are many other ways through which a person's persona is being made. We live our lives according to our persona. Many of us live the life of an ordinary person but some of us enjoy a VIP life. Human life is as beautiful as it is difficult. This book will scientifically prove that you are not just an ordinary person but a very-very important person. The best creation of God/Nature, Superhuman you are. All the 8.2 billion people are born superhumans; we all have the same software (Mind) & the same software(Body) Even science has proved this. We all humans have the power to heal ourselves, but we are not aware of this. I am a healthy 60-year-old Actor who regularly gets roles 35-45 years of age in Bollywood. By questioning the secret about my looks I shared this superhuman formula which I understood by studying the life of certified superhumans. A few of them understood it instantly, and some of them have taken their own time to understand, but Nobody has denied it. A few of them have applied it, and now they believe. their life is much healthier and wealthier. I am sure this Superhuman formula is scientifically proven, then only I am humbly sharing this idea with you now.

How did this idea come to my mind? One fine day, I watched Stan Lee's Superhumans show on the Discovery channel. Some of the world's certified superhumans participated in that show. Each one was displaying their mental or physical strength. In that particular episode, which they shot on the airport runway, certified superhuman Bill Kazsmaier, the world's strongest man, was pulling a 40-tonne Hercules Jumbo Jet with his jaw-power. I was flabbergasted by looking at the power of his jaw!

A question arose in my mind...

PART - 1

Superhuman Bill Kazsmaier

How come Bill Kazsmaier's jaw is so very strong?

He is pulling a 40 Ton Hercules jumbo jet & I get scared by breaking walnuts. I don't want my teeth broken.

Although we are both the product of love, is there any basic difference between me and him?

Then I realised Strongman Bill Kazmaier must have done practice. He must have pulled an auto first, then tempo, truck-trolley, and train engine, and then he would have pulled the jumbo jet as well. There is a saying... Practice makes a man perfect. These sayings remain for centuries. Everything has changed, but sayings still remain because sayings are the truth of the centuries. My interest developed in Superhumans' life & their life pattern, so I started my research on it.

Through science books, I studied human minds & bodies. All the certified Superhumans interviews/videos and books proved that there is no difference between certified superhumans and other humans' machines. We all humans have the same machine as iPhone 16 phones and have the same software and hardware. All the 8.2 billion humans in the world have the same software and hardware.

All the certified humans and scientists have proved that we are all born superhumans. The coronavirus vaccine will work for all humans. It's not a different vaccine for a small caste man or the other one for the upper caste. A different vaccine for a black man and another one for a white man. A different vaccine for a female and another one for a male, isn't it? According to the Guinness Book of World Records, all the certified humans who have created or broken records have done so not by those specific humans but by the human's machine only - the machine which you are also having. All the certified Superhumans have proven our machine is very strong, but Many of us are using our power a little. It's exactly the same way that we buy the best iPhone & use it to call or message only and not use its other features. The Superhumans, Scientists, Athletes, Boxers, Astronauts, and players have shown the incredible power of the human machine which proves we are all amazing. We all have superpowers within us; 4% of humans are using all their superpowers and have 76% of the total wealth of the world.

When are we going to use our minds and physical power to the fullest?

According to Stan Lee's Superhumans List, there are two Indians who have been registered as superhumans.

: Superhuman Raj Mohan Nair, The Electric Man

: Superhuman Jyothi Raj The Monkey Man

They belong to the Karnataka and Kerala states of India.

Superhuman Raj Mohan Nair
"The Electric Man"

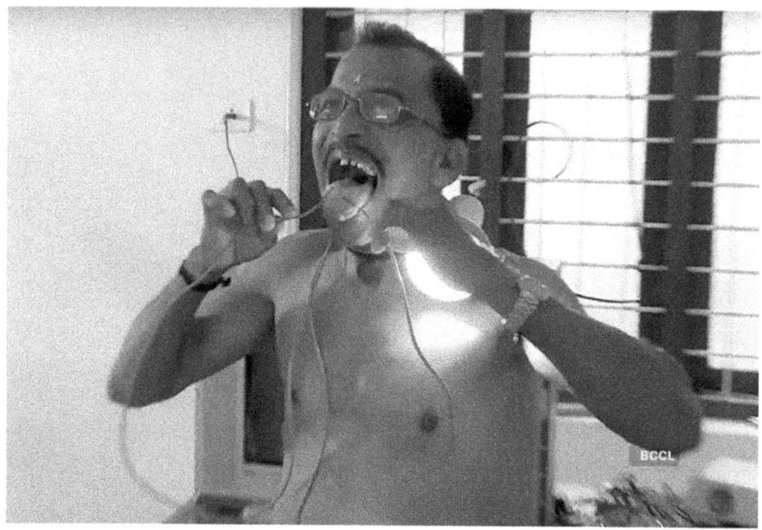

Superhuman Electric Man Raj Mohan Nair can sit on the highest voltage live wire and will not get electrocuted. He came to know this when he tried to kill himself in the past and climbed a 440-volt electrical pole but failed to kill himself. Scientists have done research on his body and found that his body is already producing lots of electricity by itself. You can use his body as a heater and make a cup of tea.

Do you think this electricity is not in your body?

Of course, it is there, same software (mind), same hardware (body).

Science has not discovered yet one day they will develop. The scientists are continuously working on it and will remain working.!

Superhuman Jyothiraj
"The Monkey Man"

Superhuman Jyothi Raj "The Monkey Man" keeps climbing on Karnataka's temples like a monkey. Jumping with speed, he has shown us the strength of a human's finger.

Are our fingers differently manufactured than his?

never - ever!

We have the same software(mind)and the same hardware (body).

Superhuman Mike Tyson

If superhuman Mike Tyson can develop his fist to the equivalent of 450 kg strength, then with practice; you can also develop your fist strength as much or even more than him. Other humans also developed this strength, just like Evander Holyfield, who knocked out Mike Tyson.

Even Though you can do it or could have done it, you have concentrated your mind and body power towards some other subject.

Superhuman Wright Brother

They also wanted to turn upside down in mid-air like other children, but they invented an airplane. They risked their lives many times but finally succeeded in flying the plane. It's a miracle! Superhumans, the Wright brothers, have invented the fastest & safest way of travelling by inventing the aeroplane. Now there are flying suits available too.

Salute to those human brains.

Every Human is a Born Superhuman

When we talk about Superheroes, we imagine characters endowed with extraordinary powers—such as the ability to fly, invisibility, or immense strength. But have you ever thought that every human, in their own way, is a superhuman? These powers may not be as cinematic or fictional, but in reality, every individual possesses unique qualities that make them exceptional. Let's explore this idea in detail.

Being superhuman is not just about physical or mental strength. It represents the ability to overcome challenges and achieve one's goals. Every person has distinct capabilities which, if recognized and nurtured, can make them extraordinary. These abilities can manifest in any field—education, arts, sports, service, or any other domain. Within every human lies an invaluable power: self-confidence. This is the force that gives them the courage to accomplish tasks that seem impossible. When a person truly believes in themselves, they can turn the impossible into reality. There are countless examples in the world that prove that every human is inherently a superhuman. As I claimed in the book that I am proving it scientifically that you are born superhuman let's check it scientifically & practically.

Evaluation of the Human S.W.O.T

Humanity is our subject. To know humans in detail, we need to do a S.W.O.T. analysis of humans. S.W.O.T. analysis is very important for any PowerPoint report.

S.W.O.T. analysis helps us to know any subject or project in detail.

S.W.O.T. analysis is used to identify the strengths and weaknesses of any project. This S.W.O.T. analysis will help us to know the capability of humans and their incompetence.

S – Strength

Which of Nature's gifts can we deny?

Nature/Creator has given us this Wonderful Human Life as well as five Senses: see, listen, smell, taste and touch. Apart from these Eishwer has given us unaccountable opportunities like Parents, Home, hunger & food, thirst and siblings, daughters even cry is for the healing. We humans have taken over the world's Land, Water & Air. We have conquered the Sea waters to navigate our Ships & the Skies; only humans can fly Planes and go to Space in a Space Jet. The Scientists are working day & night to create something new.

Nature has not given wings to humans but has given them the strength to create wings due to humans flying to space. Even eagles are not scaling as high as humans. Besides humans, there are no other creatures whose bodies are made in such a way that they can make such innovations. Since time immemorial, only Humans have changed their lives through their creations. The Creator has provided his best trait, the 'creation tool', for us. This means this globe is created especially for humans; all the religious scriptures also claim this. The highlight is that we have achieved all this when, according to science, to date, human minds have only used 11%.& 89% of our mind is still not utilised!

When are we going to start using our minds to their fullest capacity?

Simply, we can do it instantly! We can change instantly. If we change mentally, we change completely. In spite of lots of power, The Creator has blessed us with another. a very-very Special power, the power of choice. We can choose either good or bad. We can choose whether we want to live under fear or fearlessness. we can change our choice Instantly; this is the true strength!

W – Weakness

Humans are as strong as they are weak. We stumble, we die; without water, we die; lots of water, we die. Without food, we die; We die of overeating. Heart attack, TB, Coronavirus.

We also die with a knife, bullets, etc! There are millions of ways humans can die in seconds. We take the next breath; it's not in our hands but in the hands of our Creator. Humans do not have control over life & death. However, you can kill someone and save them, too. If humans had control over death, then there would be many humans who would be alive from the time this planet was discovered.

Top Ten Human Problems By Google:

1. Climate change
2. Poverty
3. Agriculture
4. Deforestation
5. Environmental issues Air
6. Air pollution
7. Terrorism & War
8. Lack of Education
9. Child Labour
10. Political Corruption

O – Opportunity

As soon as a person is born, their life is filled with countless opportunities. The taste of mother's milk, the joy of seeing, the joy of sleeping, the joy of dreaming, the joy of smiling, the family's attention,the joy of listening,the joy of speaking, joy of walking-running, joy of playing, the joy of school & joy holidays! The joy of Youthfulness, the joy of romance, the joy of college, the joy of choosing a profession! The joy of friendships. Joy of aloofness, joy of driving & swimming, joy of making money, The joy of being a Parent &Grandparents! All these joys are opportunities for us! From birth to death, humans have immense opportunities until we die! Even death is an opportunity for the Superhumans.

Why is death a gift for superhumans?

We all want to live here forever, though we all know the human body disintegrates after a certain time. Imagine if a person gets 250 years to live in this physical body. The body would disintegrate; surely, he would be pleading for the blessings of death only. That helpless person would be lying in some aloofness. He would be pleading for death only no matter how rich he is, so death is surely a gift. This life is beautiful because it ends. Peace is a must; our Creator knows the best for us. God keeps giving us opportunities but we don't show gratefulness, we don't feel gratefulness though all the religions say feel gratefulness all the time. We lose many opportunities in life by not making the correct decisions in the given time. We need to grab it at the given time while smiling.

We think we shall get these offers regularly, but that opportunity might never come back in our lifetime, and we keep talking and thinking about that offer repeatedly, but of no use. You already said NO...!!!

Now wait for the next offer which god surely will provide you then be smart & grab that opportunity with a great smile.. A dialogue from Superhuman Director Tigmanshu Dhulia's classic Movie 'Haasil'. 'Opportunity' - as small as the word is – it lasts that long only.

Our Creator/Nature is so kind; there are lots of opportunities on your way from now onwards. Grab millions-billions of opportunities.

T – Threat

Man faces only those dangers that stem from his own created fears.

Fear is a powerful emotion. If misused, it acts like a virus.

In reality, we should use fear only when we go against nature. At such times, we must truly be afraid! Those actions go against the universe and humanity. We must stop them immediately. This is why nature has instilled this emotion within us. A human being must remain emotionally balanced throughout life; this is the greatest wisdom.

As long as we are alive, we will continue to receive shocking news that shakes us. If you are young, you will inevitably hear the news of your parents passing away. If you are old, you will face health issues. If you are a businessman, you will suffer losses because both profit and loss are part of business.

Animals live their lives with complete joy. They don't know whether they will have food the next day after eating today. Yet, they do not starve like humans. From ants to hippos, all creatures find food regularly. They live fearlessly. It is the Creator's promise that He will provide us with sustenance regularly, whether we walk the path of righteousness or tread an evil path.

Do crocodiles or lions live in fear of death?

Absolutely not, though they always strive to ensure their safety.

Humans, on the other hand, are never satisfied with the food they receive. We hoard wealth for ourselves, our children, and even for the next seven generations. The richest man in the world still wants to earn more. He is also haunted by the fear of losing what he has accumulated. Fear means harming our own mind and body. Fear means that we have nurtured a virus within our minds. For instance, a soldier at the border gets wounded by an enemy bullet. He does not fear; instead, he gathers the courage to overcome his hardships and somehow reaches his base. From there, fellow soldiers take him to the hospital, where doctors remove the bullets, and he is out of danger. But a fearful person can die of a heart attack just by seeing someone brandish a knife.

Why do we keep getting scared?

Fear of losing our job, fear of health issues, fear of financial loss, fear of nuclear war, fear of civil unrest, fear of the virtual world, fear of diseases, and fear of existence itself. When we are born, we are given either a superiority complex or an inferiority complex by our parents and family. We are taught that we are the best while others are ordinary, or that we are the worst while others enjoy their lives. Life experiences show us that the people we once considered "B-grade" individuals actually outperform us. The superiority complex gradually turns into an inferiority complex. That is when fear takes root, and it is the most dangerous form of fear.

Do we want our children to grow up with fear?

We ourselves are constantly fearful for our children—what will happen to them if we die?

So, we desperately try to accumulate more and more wealth and property. We are living in fear.

We have no trust in our Creator or nature, despite the fact that we are all superhuman beings.

Top ten fears of humans:

1. Death:
A newborn dies and a 100 year old dies too. It's not a threat. Death is a reality and Why fear when it's real.

2. Losing Wealth:
The rich people always fear someone will rob them to be a popper so every Religion has specially guided us to share which increases your wealth.

3. Losing Health:
Whoever regularly abuses their body has a continuous threat to their life.It is a must to take care of your health. It's the most glorious gift for us ask rich and sick people.

4. Losing Relationship:
If we really started believing and practically applying that every person is a superhuman like yourself then our social conduct would be perfectly alright. Their life is also as important as ours and it's a proven fact. Then relationship will not be spoiled because misbehaviour is the main cause of any broken relationship. If the other people are misbehaving with you believe it they are leading a pathetic life because by keeping jealousy or abusing you they are in a loss not you.it's' wise

to be Stay away from them. Human those who respect themselves can't even disrespecting others. The respect is a foundation of any relation. If there is no respect then it's nothing. I love you, I love you, keep repeating these words is just out of habit.

5. Losing Power:

A superhit dialogue from movie Spiderman:

...with great power comes great responsibility.

Each and every powerful person is going to be powerless one day and it's a proven fact. Using power wisely until we have it.

6. Getting Insulted:

Those who disrespect others are disrespectful themselves. No one can disrespect any respectable person. Anyway getting respect or disrespect is in the hand of our Almighty.

7. Ghosts:

A human is a soul only. God's loveable soul, therefore he is always with each & every soul so why fear ghosts just throw them from our minds or enjoy them in cinema.

8. Pain:

Pain is not for suffering but for the safety otherwise during our childhood we innocent kids could have broken our finger reaching home would have been saying while laughing:

... Mama see... My finger was dismantled from my hand as I smashed a big stone on it... Please stick to them.

Pain is a unique way of diagnosing the disease and due to pain only we keep protecting ourselves. Otherwise a thief would have said to the cop while laughing:

...beat...beat me more...are you tired...give me more....

9. Accident:

Bad roads or Not being alert and arrogance are the main causes of most accidents. Arrogance is the basic problem of humans. It has another name which is Satan.

10. Violence:

Violence is really the most dangerous for human. This starts with negative thoughts & hatred language further moves toward actions. We must kill in its inception. Otherwise it could lead to viral.Yes killing for self defense and justice could be required. Arrogance is the main route cause of most of the violence.

End of S.W.O.T. analysis

Result of S.W.O.T. Analysis "Superhuman You Are"

Nature/Creator has made you the world's strongest species. Humans are superior to all living creatures. This world has been created for you only. The human mind is the creator of every science. All computers are a copy of your mind. All the engines in the world are inspired by the human mind & body. Science has been created by humans. All scientists are humans only. Nature/Creator has given the world's control to humans.

We, humans, have managed to get the lions to do acrobatics and even got elephants to blow trumpets in the Circus.

Humans have gone to space. Air, water, and sky are all under the control of humans! Humanity is the best creation of nature, so it's a scientifically proven fact that 'Superhuman You Are'. Now the question arises... **If humans are the best creation of nature/creator, why is human life so weak and frustrating?** Why is there so much dark out there?

To know the world correctly, we have to go back in a quick flashback.

Flashback starts

The Big-Bang

Big Bang Theory is a boon of science & religion.

Did the chicken come first or the egg?

Whenever this question arises, half of them mention egg and the other half mention chicken! There will be arguments, but the question still remains. Some are true, and some are false. Which one is true and which is false? Even the police cannot differentiate.

Science will give the 'correct' answer. There was love between cock and hen. The egg was conceived, and then the hen sat on the egg for a scientifically set time, or else the egg would have been spoiled. Result: The chicken came before the egg; so it's a hen scientifically proven.

In the same way as hen & the egg, 'The First Human Couple' came to this world, which is even mentioned in most of the religious scriptures. Adam & Eve loved each other and gave birth to other humans. In this loving way, the population of humans increased. Some might differ on this point, but humans were enjoying their life more naturally for a certain time.

After entering this world, all humans learned the world systems from fellow humans. Everyone has their own beliefs, their own experiences, and that's the reason why we differ from each other. The great thing is that we all humans of the world is all connected with each other. So everyone has their own belief. It's a connection of humanity.

The love increased and today we are 8.2 billion worldwide. We all were one community initially but at the age of the uninformed. Due to ignorance & differences, mugging, dacoity, murder, and rape became daily news. Humans were not aware of the concept of good or bad, a wife or a daughter. No relationships are being created except for males & females. An era of ignorance and stupidity! The atmosphere of 'Might is Right!'

When sin grows on Earth, people live in fear! And then, time by time, they, the Messengers of God were sent with the Scriptures of Religion.

The Messengers have told us who our 'Sister' is and what a 'Wife' means, who our 'Aunty' is! You have to behave like this with your wife and differently with your sister and mother. Even atheist also follow the same pattern.

Which actions are right and which are against nature, basically the social conduct.

Messengers tell you good and bad news. Slowly, people started to adopt religion and progressed to become educated human beings due to study of religion.

Religion

In today's world, there are 8–10 major religions, and 93% of people are believers. Our world should be like heaven, shouldn't it?

Only 7% of people are atheists who do not believe in any religion.

I can confidently say that this community also practices the most essential principle of religion in a practical way, which is good conduct. In fact, atheists follow religious principles more than hypocritical religious people. This clearly means that hypocritical people are not on the path of peace.

Atheists believe that there is no God, only nature. They often find it amusing when believers say that after death, after our bones decay and our existence ends, God will judge our deeds on Judgment Day. They wonder: How can anyone question us when we no longer exist?

Atheists firmly believe that this is the only life; the idea of living again is nothing but a myth. We are born here, live here, and eventually perish here.

On the other hand, religious people believe that we are made of soil and that the earth is our mother. We are born from it, and in its embrace, we rest forever. Science also confirms that the minerals found in the earth are present in our bodies, and the water composition of our bodies matches that of the earth.

Whether we are cremated or buried after death, we merge with the earth. When this short life ends, our next life—an eternal one—begins. Just like a movie has a short teaser, this life is a teaser for our eternal life.

"Picture abhi baaki hai, mere dost"—The full story is yet to come.

This life is a test for us!

Is your Allah a filmmaker who created us for mere entertainment?

No doubt, your question is profound and thought-provoking. The Creator did not make this world for entertainment but to establish the victory of truth over falsehood. Every day, every moment, our life is a test.

Wealth and poverty both serve as tests:

- The wealthy are tested by how they use their resources.
- The poor are tested by whether they remain honest or resort to lies and deceit for survival.

If God controls everything, doesn't He already know what people will do? Then why this test?

Indeed, God knows everything, but He also granted humans **Free Will**—the freedom to choose between right and wrong. This freedom itself makes life a test.

Imagine a teacher who can predict which students might pass or fail. Yet, the examination is still conducted to ensure fairness. Would it be just to pass or fail students without giving them a chance to prove themselves?

Similarly, those who murder innocent people and those who dedicate their lives to serving humanity cannot meet the same end. Can we treat **Hitler** and **Mother Teresa** equally?

No, we cannot!

Hitler killed over **6 million** innocent people—can his single death compensate for such a horrific crime?

This means **justice is pending**. Judgment Day will surely come.

There must be another world where:

- The wicked will face the full consequences of their deeds—enduring unimaginable suffering.
- The righteous, who spent their lives helping others, will enjoy eternal peace and bliss.

This is what all religious scriptures and divine messengers have conveyed for centuries.

The Messengers of God

Who Are These Messengers?

Whenever sin increases on Earth, and falsehood becomes widespread, The Creator sends a Messenger to guide humanity. Messengers teach people how to live righteous lives and instill good morals and proper conduct.

In ancient times, when ignorance and immorality spread in India, and falsehood reached its peak, with atrocities and violence becoming common, God sent Shri Ram to India. Being a king superhuman Shri Ram lived a life full of suffering to demonstrate that God is Truth. Many people believed his words and began living virtuous lives. However, Shri Ram's message could not reach the rest of the world because there was no internet at that time.

God's concern isn't limited to India alone; He desires to improve the lives of all humanity. When ignorance grew in Jerusalem, The Creator sent Messenger Jesus to Bethlehem, who guided the misguided people there and taught them proper morals. Later, when ignorance spread in the Arab lands, Allah sent Messenger Muhammad (s.a.w) to guide the people. All Messengers—whether Shri Ram, Moses, Jesus, Guru Nanak, Buddha, Mahavira,Confucius and Muhammad (s.a.w)— came for the benefit of all humanity, not just a specific region. The messages of all these Messengers emphasise peace and good conduct.

Today, with humanity's scientific progress, we can practically follow the teachings of our beloved Messengers and spread their messages globally through the internet.

Why are Messengers humans and not angels because you got angles too?

Messengers are human to prove that this life is a test. If an angel delivered God's message, all humanity would instantly believe, and the test of life would end on the same day.

Some religions consider their Messengers as God, but not all do. How?

No Messenger has ever claimed to be God or a form of God. All Messengers worshipped The Creator, which itself proves that they were Messengers and not God. "No one but Satan desires to be worshipped." This misunderstanding stems from the human ego.In the eyes of nature, all humans are equal—no one is superior or inferior; otherwise, our physical and mental makeup would not be the same. What makes someone great or small depends on their actions.

If you belong to religion A, does that make followers of religions B, C, or D inferior? This is false! We, as religious individuals, have decided our religion is the supreme religion, while others are categorised as bad religions.

Why does Satan have control over humans in every religion?

Satan exists as a tool to test human hearts and minds; otherwise, how could life be a test? Even the ability to take a life is a test allowed by God because it determines whether a person passes to the next level. If this ability didn't exist, God wouldn't have created humans with the capacity to harm each other. God is immensely merciful. A person who unjustly takes another's life fails their test, while the one whose life was taken passes and enters eternal bliss if he lived a superhuman life. We have a free will that allows humans to choose between a positive path or a negative one influenced by Satan.

The Gist of All Religions

The similarity of all religions:

It's the need of the hour. We must understand the similarities of religion and finish personnel enmity.

If you study Comparative Religion, you will find maximum similarities in the spiritual books of all religions and the similarity of teaching social conduct only by many different messengers. They all are saying, "Stay peaceful, be with truth, don't harm anyone, stealing, raping, and killing are the worst crimes; stay away from them." How can any other prophet be fake if he is preaching the same? Even killing is possible due to testing otherwise, nature will never allow any human to be killed by another human. He is so merciful. The person who kills fails in his exam. If the dead person is innocent, he will surely be passed and continue to enjoy his eternal life. Through free will, humans can spend their lives positively or the devil's way negatively.

Once we pass, we shall get the things that are great for us. What are the Top Ten desires of humans in this World at present? Almighty/Nature would provide us with these things to the fullest after we pass this life test. Non-believers may think, "What is the reason for God testing us when He knows what anyone will become in this life, a killer or a saviour?"

You religious people claim that not even a leaf can be unturned without The Creator's wish, so the question arises: where do we have free will? If a killer is killing someone, it's the will of our God. How could a killer kill without God's permission? So where is free will & why would that killer be punished?

Does our Creator not know, well in advance, what all humans are supposed to do in their lives? Why does God not punish directly? What is the use of this life test?

First of all we can't question our creator why have you done that & why haven't you done that? if you can please keep trying. Life is a Test. If you are Rich or Poor, it's a test! How do you behave as a Rich man, where you have spent your Money is a test. Or if you are Poor, what would you do to survive: steal, kill, or do hard work and enjoy it? Look at this Universe as a live movie created by Nature/Almighty. The Screenplay is written by Nature/Creator, & You are the Protagonist of Nature's live movie & Satan is the main Negative Character. In this nature's live movie, our Creator has narrated the whole Script in his many Holy Scriptures, so we must understand the Story-Screenplay very well.

To give a good performance any actor demands the script of the movie to play the role but we don't want to read God's script and blame God for punishing us unnecessarily. He sends many Messengers to direct us to the right path. We have free will, so we can adopt characteristics of Nature/Almighty or Satan's. Suppose a 93-year-old Terrorist goes to a School and kills 500 Students by planting lethal Bombs in their School;

then the Terrorist dies Naturally without being caught. Is justice done, or has to be done?

Justice surely remains! This means there must be another world where justice would be served; otherwise, if we are killing each other right now, and that is fine, let's do it faster. Religions have only told us how to behave. Humanity is only told by the messengers. Humanity is itself a religion. This is the crux of all religions. One person who spent his life improving another's life, while a person has killed many innocent people, are both the same? Forget about God. Are they the same in your system? What are you going to do if you are a creator? Do you see the Natural system imbalanced? Will you or nature just leave these killers free? Is nature not scientifically correct?Do you find any defect or imbalance in this beautiful Nature?

All the messengers have come used to eating food and roam in the markets. If The Creator sends an angel, then all humans will listen to that angel immediately. Then what will happen to the life test? It will end the same day! Just like our happiness, others' happiness too. Like others' pain, there is our pain, too. Each and every life is very important. If one innocent person is killed by somebody, it's as bad as killing the whole universe. Every individual is a complete universe in itself! Though killing for justice is justified. If we study the life of any twin brothers/sisters, both lives will be very different because both are individually unique. Similarly, you, too, are unique and a complete universe. If all humans were with the same face height, it would have been a mess.

Imagine you are The Creator of this World. You have created 8.2 billion robots and not humans. Those robots who do not follow your commandments or social conduct, Those who massacre other robots, those who do not let others live peacefully. Will you not punish those terrorist robots? Would you not give prizes to the well-conducted robots? Nature loves all. We are one & our Creator is one... Our Creator does not look like a human. He is a source of energy. There is only & There is only one Creator possible.

There cannot be so many Khuda otherwise, they would have fought among themselves. Even in today's time, there's always one Chief, only one Chief in a Village, one Chief in the State, and one Chief in the Country. If there were two Prime Ministers or two Presidents, they would fight within themselves only. If there were many Creators, then every Creator would have taken his force and attacked others. We must see our machine (The mind & body) coming from one factory only.

Surely, we have one Creator. We are one & our Creator is One!!!

What actually happened in the past...

People have started loving their Messenger to the extent of blindness, and they have started praying to them, believing that they were incarnations of God, though no Messenger has ever told people, "I am God." They always said, "I am the Messenger of God." God doesn't need to sleep; He does not require food, and He never exhausts because he is not human. He created the first human, then more humans. He is not human or looks like a human. He is The Nature, The Energy. We blindly believe he must be looking like a human. He is not human, so he does not have a Parent or son. If he has Parents, the Parents are bigger. If he has a Son, the Son is the future. He does not need to be incarnated as a human and go to the washroom for nature calls. He is Nature Himself. He says, "Be it so be it." He decides the screenplay of the whole Universe. Imagine you are The Creator who has created the whole Universe: the Moon, The Sun, Stars, and Galaxies & you are going to the toilet & having constipation. Can you imagine? He does not need water to survive. He doesn't require sleep or food because he is not human. Probably the way we religious people believe the tortoise community must be thinking the same way: God must be the biggest tortoise!!! The creator is formless. God is energy, the source of energy, nature.

Those who preach about truth & decent social conduct are all good; none of They are bad. Religion can never be bad. For any religion, blind faith is fake; even all the spiritual books have guided us to study first, then to believe. Each one believes in science. We must go scientifically; humans must check what they are following.

Does your religion make you violent or a killer?

All the messengers have guided us to the right path; they all are true messengers without a single doubt. All the messengers used to roam around and eat like us only. They all preach peace so no one could be bad. Imagine they all are meeting at a cafe. What would they be fighting or respecting each other?

They all have the same job. All the books say those worshippers who follow their messengers are the best. All the messengers' social conduct was peaceful in their most difficult life. These are a few mixed Commandments of Messengers like Buddha, Moses, Ram & Muhammad. May peace be upon him. Could you identify which commandment is from which religious messenger?

1. "Be plain and simple to be identical with Nature."
2. "Be truthful. Take miseries as a divine blessing for your own good and be thankful."
3. "You should not misuse the name of your Lord, the God. For the Lord will not hold anyone guiltless who misuses His name."
4. "Honour your father and your mother so that you may live long in the land the Lord your God is giving you."
5. "You shall not murder."
6. "Do not come near indecencies, openly or secretly. You shall not commit adultery."
7. "You shall not steal."
8. "Tell no lies and deceive no one."
9. "Do not take what is not given to you."
10. "You shall not give false testimony against your neighbour."
11. "You shall not covet your neighbour's house. You shall not covet your neighbour's wife, or his male or female servant, his ox, or donkey, or anything that belongs to your neighbour."

12. "Know all the people as thy brethren and treat them as such."
13. "Be not revengeful for the wrongs done by others. Take them with gratitude as heavenly gifts."
14. "Mould your living so as to rouse a feeling of love and piety in others."
15. "At bedtime, feeling the presence of God, repent for the wrong committed unknowingly. Beg forgiveness in a supplicant mood, resolving not to allow repetition of the same."

This is the base for all religions. The end result for every Religion is The height of social conduct. If anyone speaks very badly to you, you need to speak very well in return – just see, he will become your 'true friend'. We think only repeating rituals is real worship. These following actions are also an act of worship apart from rituals we adhere to." If you take care of yourself, you are doing an act of worship. If you are taking care of your family, it's an act of worship. If you are working for yourself and your family, it's an act of worship. If you are calm, it's an act of worship. If you are doing something for society, it's an act of worship. If you are a farmer, it's an act of worship. If you are a sweeper, It's an act of worship. If you are doing something for stray dogs/cats, it's an act of worship. If you are sleeping at the right time, it's an act of worship. When there is so much similarity in all religions, then why are we fighting for it? Ignorance is the basis of all fights. Initially, we were all one community but due to ignorance & differences, people were divided into many tribes. The virus of ignorance spoils our social conduct. Though for the Nature/Creator, all humans are equal! No one is below us and no one is above us,only our deeds are important. Historically & truthfully, we have decided ourselves that we belong to the A category, the best one & the oldest one. While others are from the B, C, D, X, Y, and Z categories. If people from religion A believe their religion is the best, then they must want people from other religions to follow their religion because your religion must be more peaceful; that's why you are calling them to peace. Peacefully, not forcefully, because forcing is banned in all religions. Calling other humans to my religion peacefully means I must want betterment in others' lives & afterlife. This means we religious humans want other humans to be saved from Hellfire. That's the biggest sign that **'Superhuman You are'**.

Besides your religion A people, the rest of the people in the world become your clients automatically. If we are really religious, we must feel that our religion should be spread everywhere for the betterment of humanity, for the whole of humanity. Achieve heaven for fellow humans & live in heaven eternally. Actually, we all want to sell our religion to others to make money and gain power. We are not good salesmen despite believing. Customers are a form of God. That's what is written in many shops in India. Everyone values their clients, or do they do ethnic cleansing of them? We must be the most humble community on this Earth because the rest of the humans are our raw stock. Otherwise, who are we going to get reverted or converted if we kill them all? It must be done through God's way only. Peaceful. Humbly Yours, Style! How Can any good salesman crack a better deal compared to his fellow salesmen?

He must be humble and presentable for sure in comparison! We have to behave like good salesmen if we are selling our religion. We all believe our religion is the best product. Money-Power, plus Heaven Eternally!

Due to the laziness of the so-called followers of religion, they never felt the need to read their scriptures. Even those who did read them often relied on translations in languages they didn't fully understand, leading to a failure to grasp the true meaning of their texts and their Messenger's message. We began following religious intermediaries instead of directly connecting with their faith. These intermediaries—religious 'contractors'—distorted the essence of religion and turned it into a business. They divided a single truth into numerous religions.

We are one and our creator is one.

The Mediator

We all believe that only our religion is best & the other one is worst. Due to laziness we did not feel any need to read our holy book. The people read it could not understand because they all were in different languages. They did not understand the messages of their respective messengers. It was easy to run behind any person who claimed I have read it all & you may ask me anything. We created a mediator between God and us. Agent will surely teach you religion according to their well beings. They made one religion into many religions. Mediators will teach religion according to their own will, the business religion.

Are mediators better than us? Do they have a direct connection with The Creator, and do we not? Although they and we have the same software and hardware, Every government office has a notice board stating 'Beware of Agents'! Still, we prefer to go to the agents because of our laziness. All the Prophets/Messengers have conveyed that you and God have a direct connection, and there is strictly no mediator. If there are agents, there is a hierarchy. When those following religion A, their scholar found that there was another Prophet who appeared in Bethlehem, so they got scared to lose their respect, money & power. They denied Jesus as a messenger of The Creator. The reason given was that his clothes are different, his language is different, his book is different. He is a liar, and we are the best.

Although The message from the Prophet Jesus is also the same **decent social conduct** for humanity,

Exactly as given by the messenger of religion (A). Similarly, followers of Bethlehem said we are the best.

Those following religion A are godless, their dresses are different, their books are different, etc., etc.!

Those following religion C said, "We are the best; B and A are bad!"

Those Messengers who teach that 'Truth will Triumph' are definitely correct, irrespective of which religion they come from, even if they were the first or have come later. They have the same message:

Love is God. When these religious leaders heard about another Prophet named Jesus in Bethlehem, they rejected him outright without understanding his message or reading his scriptures. This rejection was driven solely by personal interests, even though Jesus's message was the same as that of their own messengers:

God is Truth. Similarly, the religious leaders in Bethlehem told their followers that they were supreme and that those who came before or after were ungodly. Leaders of religion A claimed their superiority and labelled the followers of religion B as sinners. Now think for a moment: how can any messenger be false when all of them teach the victory of truth, discourage lies, and prohibit oppression, theft, murder, and exploitation? Clearly, all of them are truthful; none of them can be false.

When Muhammad (saw) arrived in the Gulf, the religious leaders of Moses' and Jesus' followers rejected him blindly, even though his teachings were the same as those of Jesus.

The last Messenger was sent for the entire world, not just a specific place or group, because by then humanity had advanced scientifically. In today's era, any message can be spread globally in seconds through the internet. But arrogance and blindness have created a major problem: we have abandoned God because He is not visible to us. Instead, we have started worshipping saints, shrines, and tombs, imagining that God resembles a human.

Religion is a Business

A Popular Dialogue from Superhuman Super Star Shahrukh Khan's Movie 'Raees'... My mother used to say no job is small. And there is no bigger Religion is better than a job!

Robbery is the religion of Robbers; they are very religious people, and the robber thinks he's fine and The Police are bad. The religion of Drug Dealers is their work. For Contract killer Killing is his religion. Terrorists, too, are very, very religious. United Nations Chief, American President, World Bank Chief, Gangsters of the World, KGB, CIA, and ISI all follow their respective religions, their work religion. Due to so many religious human beings, so many WHYs are raised!!!

Why are Rapist-Killers set free from Jail?

Why are innocent children bombed?

Why is water depleting?

Why are neighbouring countries enemies of each other?

Why can't tobacco be banned, due to which millions of people are dying?

Why are 8 - 10 people living in one room, despite there being lots of space in the world?

Why World Atomic Countries... do not use the power of the atomic bomb for the upliftment of people?

Why does one set of humans fear their mafia and live a life of fear?

Why, in one country, is the life of humans dictated by the king, by a single human?

Why, with the support of the United Nations, do the strong countries dominate the smaller countries?

Why is there a mafia everywhere?

At home Mafia mother-in-law and mafia daughter-in-law, there are robberies on the streets, the robbery mafia. In the business, corporate mafia! Politics, Education Mafia, Land-Mafia, religion mafia! Is there a Mafia in Science too? Where there are Humans, there is business. Wherever there is Business, There has to be a mafia! Science mafia handled by political mafia & political; mafia is handled by religious mafia.

To attain Money and Power, a few Scientists manufacture Banned Drugs. These are not Scientists; they are science mafia! All Discoveries in Science should be for the Healthy-Wealthy. Life of humans and not for exploding humans with Bombs. While Science is progressing, there are very lethal Bombs being invented. Bombs are made by the mafia only. There are Special Bunkers for the World's Top-Most Leaders and their families. That's the irony: World Leaders will blast the atomic bomb on us and our families, and they themselves and their families will hide in the Bunkers! Bravo!

Has God handed over our lives to the Mafia Gang?

Who are the world's top mafia heads? Britishers? Israelis?Nepalese or Bhutanese? Americans or Iranians? Pakistanis? Saudi Arabians? Or From Other Religions? Which religion?

Actually, due to our own negativity, we have handed over our lives into the 'hands' of others. Though all our respective messengers told us that oppressing someone or being oppressed is the same.

We don't want to listen to our Messengers as we are business-minded hardcore Religious lazy humans out of this just check our social justice.

The Social Justice

Today if a Rich man's Son rapes and murders a Poor girl, he would go to India's best advocate after committing this crime! The rapist would confess to the top advocate in detail about his heinous crime. Why doesn't the top-most advocate immediately inform the judge and get the criminal punished?

With evidence, of course! Law asks for evidence only, but the advocate will declare in the court that his Client is Innocent. A law graduate advocate will also prove that his client was admitted to a hospital in another town at the time of the crime for flu or high blood pressure.

Heated arguments would continue, and Finally, that human-shaped devil, the rapist, the killer, is acquitted!

The next day, the headlines on the front page of the newspaper carry this: "Rape and Murder Accused Mr. X has been acquitted freely by the top-most advocate!" Media impacts other humans; there is an increase in the number of rapes and murders! An advocate is a staunch religious person, besides being a law graduate. Business is his religion. If a rape/murder occurred with the daughter of the lawyer, then what would happen?

Would the lawyer protect the rapist/killer? Would he be acquitted free? Definitely not! After winning the case, the top advocate will have a grand party at a 5-star hotel or at his expensive farmhouse! Those humans who are invited to the party would be proud that they have been invited by such a well-known lawyer. Relatives/friends of the advocate will bring flowers & gifts to praise him to the skies, and possibly, parents would want their child to be an Assistant to the Lawyer and would also click their selfies!

The Central Government will also praise this Promising Lawyer in the coming years. This lawyer will be elected as a Law Minister! Who else will be more suitable than him?

Imagine if the victim girl were the daughter of advocate would he have helped the rapist & killer to get scot free?

Never-ever.

It was somebody else's daughter and the accused was his friend's son. The advocate is a graduate of lawplus he is a very religious man.Rapists, Advocates, Media, Silent public like us have Multiplied the Negative Energy in the Universe. There won't be any difference in the lives of decent people! Our entire generation of Literate humans will silently and lovingly accept that justice was done, and everything was done in the purview of law! We all want World peace! What about the victim girl? If she were our sister-daughter?!

We can't even imagine.

Hatred

Hatred has a unique characteristic—it continues to grow, but our numbers keep dwindling. We, the religious people, are busy plotting against each other's existence. Most of us believe that by doing so, we earn virtue and assist God in eradicating sin from the earth. Our God desires this, and God belongs only to us. We are merely eliminating the demonic people! The consequences of hatred include nuclear bombs, chemical weapons, poisonous gases and other viruses!

We must eliminate hatred at its very root. Only four percent of the world's population holds the majority of wealth, and these four percent have enslaved the rest of humanity. They do not want all people to be healthy and prosperous. They know that human existence depends on ideology. We have not yet utilized the full capacity of our brains, and that is why they have enslaved the rest of humanity. The villains of the world have turned our lives into hell.

Who are these people responsible for our current situation?

The great Scientist Albert Einstein once said:

"This world is not a bad place because some villains spread evil. This world is a bad place because the rest of the people do nothing about it."

If only 0.2 percent of the world's 8.2 billion population are villains, then what are the remaining 8 billion people doing?

Hatred...

Hatred in the heart, hatred in the body, Hatred for the mere existence of others.

And one more special thing about hatred— It burns the one who harbors it.

Those whom you hate are savoring the flavors of life, While you have set your own heart on fire,

Running your engine with the handbrake on— Burnout is inevitable. Believe it or not, most humans, knowingly or unknowingly, are engaged in wiping each other out. I am not saying this about you, but rather about the traitors of the world who have turned our lives into hell.

Superhuman Peter Macwilliam

Said... **"Your mind cannot afford the luxury of a negative thought."**

In his book, 'The Life 101 Series', Peter McWilliams has scientifically proved. Just like a single virus can damage our computer/mobile, exactly a virus can also damage our brain. In our mind, there are lots of viruses all the time which create fear, the biggest virus. Not a single negative thought. Superhuman they are, superhuman we are, superhuman 'You' are, stay enlightened!!!

Every day, we have to watch our daily schedule, from the time we wake up to the time we get back to bed. We need to enjoy life on a daily basis because tomorrow never comes. The humans we meet need to treat them as Superhumans. Whoever we meet, we need to believe in our hearts that he/she is a Superhuman. Every individual has a complete universe for himself, and he needs breathing space. If we try to enter someone else's Universe, then they will be anxious. In the same way, if anyone tries to enter our Universe, they will repent. We consider ourselves to be the most important, and that's how we should think for others, too. You are Most Important. If anyone else finds himself as Most important, then we feel bad; they are the same as you are!!!

All those great achievers in the Universe who have been there had peaceful minds, and hence, they could achieve their goals! This mind & body are your gadgets & our slave, too. The way we take care of our mobile/computer, we need to take even more care of our mind-body. It always depends on what we feed into our mind & body. Whatever you have achieved till now is all because of your body and mind! Whatever you want to achieve in the future, you will be able to do it with your body and mind only. Basically we are slaves of our negative thoughts.

Slavery

Who are those who want to make us their slaves, and why?

If you or your family members have this option, then what will you do? Imagine my family! If my family gets this power, they can make all other humans of the world their slaves. Will my family members deny it? Definitely not. Who doesn't want Money and Power? In this World, there are Miss World, Mister Universe, Reserve Bank Manager, Scientists, Doctors, Good looking Humans, Bouncers,Home Ministers, Pole Dancers, Financiers, Film Stars, Gorgeous Models, and Housewives! Humans are the best assets, and all these humans will be Slaves to our family! Wow! Will our Family not make the other humans their Slave? We will definitely enslave everyone! Wonderful! Give us one chance, please!

As you know, We have to erase all Sins from the Earth. Practically, if we see, in today's World, Wives want their Husbands to be their Slaves. Husbands want their Wives to be their slaves. Mother-in-law wants daughter-in-law to be a slave, and daughter-in-law wants the mother-in-law to be her Slave. Parents want to enslave their children, and children want to enslave their Parents. We humans are busy trying to enslave others 24/7. These 4% of humans are also trying to keep the rest of us as Slaves. The reason is the same - Virus number ONE! In their minds, too, they have the same virus, and they are the best race. Besides their own race,they believe all humans are animals! To make animals their slaves is the birthright of humans.

Just like we put a rein in a horse's mouth and ride it, that is the right for humans!

The problem is when all other humans 'want to enslave themselves' and help them in doing so. How?

By keeping multiple viruses in their mind and by Overthinking. Most humans are living the life of a 'slave'. Slave of our thoughts! We humans live unnaturally, but all animals can live naturally because they do not have the virus called arrogance.

Arrogance: most humans have this arrogance virus in their minds, which is the main reason we are not living Superhuman lives but living the lives of ordinary humans. My life, my height, My house, My style, My face, My body, My girlfriend, My phone, My bedroom, My hair, and My voice are the best, and you are just okay types. It is true that you and everything belonging to you are the best because you are superhuman. But the rest of the humans in your circle are not as good as you are. That's our virus, and we know that too. Still, we want to be in the dark and believe otherwise. This wrong belief surely will give us multiple viruses in our brains, like overconfidence. A superiority complex will turn into an inferiority complex later on and a lack of confidence, which will create fear in our lives. Living with lies will ruin our lives. Ignorance time is here again. Slowly, we put multi-virus gangs in our minds.

Negative thinking, fear, arrogance, anger, Hate, jealousy, inferiority complex, superiority complex, and many more!

Secret Society

It is seen that there are some villains in this world who have made a Secret Society. Humans from all religions are members of this society. If such a society exists, then there is a reason for this society, and that reason is Virus number One: Ignorance, which is prevalent in everyone's mind. They think they are the best and the rest of the people are demons! These are the same humans who believe they are God's favourites.

They think that Nature/Creator has made them the most Powerful. They can utilize their Power as per their will. Few humans control the whole world's power and money & they are the world's Treasurers. In our Globe, there are banks that take care of the world's biggest criminals' money. The United Nations do not have the guts to take action against them. No one has the guts to touch them. They are untouchable types; otherwise, all countries can collectively bomb these Banks.

Why is there no lock on the banks that fund terror? These bankers are kingmakers. All the kings and ministers of the whole world are puppets in their hands. Presently, the financial situation is such that these banks have all the money from all humans across the world. This means that if it's in the bank, it is with other humans. The world works on the cashier's planning.

Business-minded religious humans like us only run this secret society which they have established. Their planning is such that we kill each other, and they will sit and watch the real-life human drama. It's all just because of their arrogance only. The highlight is that we all are fully supporting this secret society.

How?

By not using our minds 100%, making ourselves their slaves. That's what they wanted! Out of so much hate in so many minds, it does lead to a civil war!

Civil War

Civil War or Internal Conflict:

A civil war is a situation where citizens of a country engage in large-scale fighting and violence among themselves. This usually occurs when deep social inequality, communal tensions, economic crises, or political instability reach their peak.

Causes of Civil War:

1. Religious or Communal Tensions: Growing hostility between people of different religions or communities.
2. Economic Inequality: The widening gap between the rich and the poor.

3. Political Instability: Rebellion against the government or conflicts between political parties.
4. Scarcity of Resources: Severe shortages of essentials like water, food, or wealth.
5. External Interference: Provocation by other countries or organizations.

Consequences of Civil War:

- Massive Loss of Life and Property: Thousands to millions of people may die.
- Economic Devastation: The country's economy can collapse completely.
- Social Division: Hatred and divisions in society will deepen.
- Humanitarian Crisis: Hunger, poverty, displacement, and refugee crises.
- Weakened Nation: The country may become vulnerable and insecure against external enemies.

Solutions:

To prevent civil war, the government, society, and every individual must remain vigilant:

- Resolve Issues Through Dialogue and Consensus.
- Ensure Equality and Justice in Society.
- Prevent Hate Speech and Extremist Ideologies.
- Provide Economic Security and Facilities for the Poor and Underprivileged.
- Increase Education and Awareness so that people act wisely. Preventing civil war is essential for every nation and society, as it brings nothing but destruction.

Hypothetical Scenario: A Financial Meltdown Imagine if the World Bank suddenly announced that its system had been hacked, and all accounts were frozen. Restoring the system could take months. Where would people get money for their daily food? We get restless if we miss just one meal. How would people satisfy their hunger in such a situation?

The rich might survive for a few days, but perhaps not for more than a week. After that, starving people would come out onto the streets. The streets would be filled with armed mobs looting the homes and bungalows of the wealthy. As millions of hungry people take to the streets, they will not only loot but also resort to violence. Even the police will be searching for food for their own families. Markets will have nothing left to sell; all shops will be looted. Those who find nothing will, in frustration, set shops and homes on fire. This scenario has been repeatedly observed across the world.

Now, imagine if the World Bank declared today that its banking system had been hacked and a hacker had frozen all accounts. Restoring the system might take a long time. Where would people get money for their daily needs?

We become anxious if we don't get food for a single meal. What will happen if people don't get food for two or three meals in a day? The rich might stay safe for a while, but at most for a week. Then, the poor and starving masses will come out of their homes onto the streets. From the streets, they will become armed mobs and storm the houses of the wealthy. When they knock on your door, what will you do?

How long will this Republican system survive?

For every bite of food, brothers will kill brothers, husbands will kill wives—within just a week of starvation, humans will turn into beasts. Now, even the World Bank alone has the power to trigger a civil war Or imagine if the internet were shut down for six months— no money transfers, no online transactions. What then? What if the internet was permanently shut down? We don't care about reality, yet religious groups are busy deciding how many pieces people of other faiths should be cut into. Most prophets have already foretold what the future holds.

This is a serious issue, and to prevent such chaos in society, we need to unite and ACT for solutions together.

World War 3

On a golden night, if the president of a rival country drops a nuclear bomb on us, what will happen?

If they actually press the button?

Our beautiful world is always hanging by the threat of a nuclear bomb. Wicked people have built bunkers for themselves and their children, while deadly bombs are hanging over our heads and our children's heads. In this small world, so many dangerous bombs exist. If these bombs explode where they are kept, then?

Boom... boom... boom...

After that, only a few humans will survive in this vast universe! The rest will be dead! According to science, many species of cockroaches will survive.

What should we do to avoid this devastation?

No one person should have the authority to press a button and start World War III. Now, imagine, a single person has the power to destroy the entire world in an instant – a kind of superpower. Just like you.

If that happens, then what?

We don't even have an insurance policy! Now, what should I do to ensure that I, my children, my family, and my friends survive? In other words, my little world, "my world!"

If World War III occurs, we will all try to protect ourselves from toxic gases, attempt to neutralize biological weapons, hide from artillery, protect ourselves from fire, and crawl on the ground, praying for just one thing.

Peace... peace... peace.

Only peace will be wished for...

Then,

Why not peace now?

In your mind, peace means world peace. Otherwise, we'll have to blame others for unrest for the rest of our lives. Those are the traitors – they are the traitors – while the slogans echo in your own mind, but they cause no harm to those you call villains.

The Villain

Which humans are the enemies of humanity? A list of suspected humans is presented below: World's Richest Humans?

World Leaders?

United Nations?

Politicians?

Drug Dealers? Secret Society?

Pimps?

Advocates?

Doctors?

Thieves- Dacoits?

Actors?

Music Directors?

Pickpockets Or then Traffic Police?

Film World?

Agents?

Professors?

Tailors?

Carpenters?

Engineers?

Scientists?

Farmers?

People from lower caste?

People from the upper caste?

Surely! From other religions! Which religion?

People from a 'bad' religion?

There is a 'bad' religion; why wasn't I told earlier?

Is it possible that there is a 'bad' religion?

Are these people from the 'bad' religion real villains?

Superhuman Pope Jorge Mario Bergoglio

Said, "When No One is to blame, Everyone has to be blamed!"

The Villains of the world are afraid of one thing. Humans should not be able to use their Superpowers! 4-5% of humans use their Mind then it's fine, but if 100% of humans use their Super Powers, then what will happen to us?

Those who have enslaved our minds know that everything depends on the minds of humans. Catch them young and watch them grow.

That's the reason why they fill in violence in video games with our enlightened children. If there has been violence instilled in our minds from childhood, we will be mentally violent and will not even think of our own superpowers! Most video games have this format. If you kill 100 humans only, then you will reach the next level. On the next level, you only have to kill 200 humans, and then you will go to the third level. From childhood, we have been prepared for civil war. By virtually killing humans, children are happy. Virtuality is changed to reality. They have a practice of killing right from the start. Real killings are not difficult later on. If there are mass killings anywhere in the world, there are people who also party for this reason.

Who are the killers? Humans.

Whom are they killing? Humans!

Who is enjoying others' suffering? Humans!!!

The Law of Attraction

According to the Superhuman Scientist Sir Isaac Newton's law, every action (force) in nature has an equal and opposite reaction. The way we humans are collectively spreading negativity in the universe, and when we get it back in our life, then we cry of injustice! Whatever humans desire is already present within us. Currency, gold, cars, and property are all part of the planet and all made from this Earth, so we are. We just have to attract those things which we desire, and they will come to us magnetically.We must know about the Law of Attraction. In the New Thought Philosophy, the Law of Attraction is based on the belief that positive or negative thoughts bring positive or negative experiences into a person's life. The belief is based on the idea that people and their thoughts are made from 'pure energy' and that a process of energy attracts like energy, which exists through which a person can improve their health, wealth, and personal relationships. Advocates generally combine cognitive reframing techniques with affirmations to replace limiting or self-destructive "negative thoughts" with creative visualisation of more empowered, adaptive 'positive' thoughts. A component of the philosophy is the idea that in order to effectively change one's negative thinking patterns, one must also 'feel' (through creative visualisation) that the desired changes have already occurred. This combination of positive thought and positive emotion is believed to allow one to attract positive experiences and opportunities by achieving resonance with the proposed energetic law. Supporters of the Law of Attraction refer to scientific theories and use them as arguments favoring it. **Ignorance is the one and only problem for humans.** Most humans have the ignorance virus in their minds. The first virus byproduct is a lie, Ignorance + Lie, a double whammy in our minds.

Collective energy:

For example, look at a plastic ball. In the process of making the ball, plastic has been made into small pieces, then the pieces are melted at a particular temperature and then dipped in a 'dye' which makes the ball.

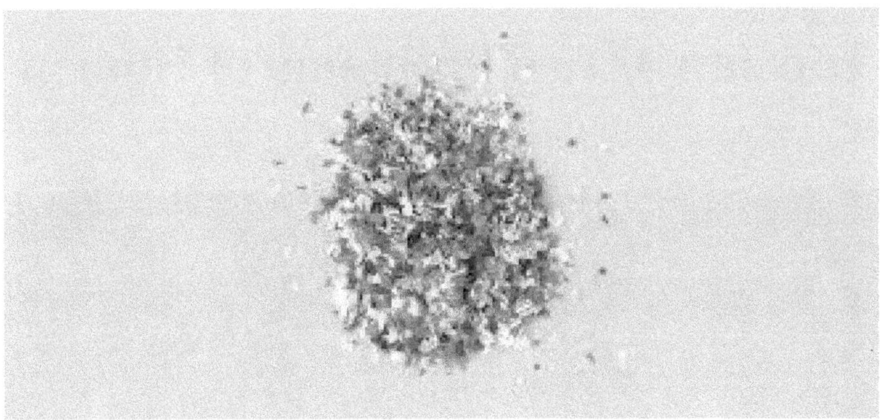

Similarly, today the entire globe's mentality is the result of all our collective thoughts. The mind is so very powerful.

Today's present condition in the world is the result of every human's collective negative energy. I am equally responsible for spreading my part of the negative energy. Just like this, the mindset of today's world is the result of all our collective thoughts. The human mind is so powerful that the current state of the world is the outcome of each individual's collective energy. If more and more of us live a life full of positive energy then the positive energy will spread more in the universe, and human life will certainly improve. And from KaliYuga, we will eventually transition into SatyaYuga.For now, let's push KaliYuga away!

Top Ten Actual Problems of Human

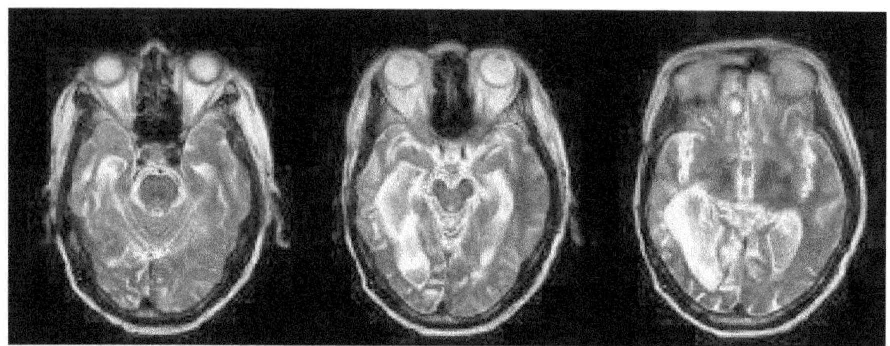

All these problems are self-created because we humans misuse our emotions.

1. Arrogance
2. Lies
3. Confusion
4. Backbiting
5. Hatred
6. Jealousy
7. Violence
8. Fear
9. Waste of energy
10. Blind faith

Flashback ends.

PART - 2

Happy Birthday to You

Love reached its peak, and that is how we are 8.2 billion humans today on the Gorgeous Globe. Love is increasing our population. There is a lot of strength in this love, which has also given life to you. From your embryonic period, your religion, career, choices, and food are all planned by some other human being. When we are born, we do not have any choice. We can neither choose our parents nor our gender, nor country, city, religion, sibling, nor teachers. Even our cousins are already there - Readymade! When we are 5-6 days old, we laugh and cry as per our free will. We have a fresh mind without any virus & we live a superhuman life.

As we grow older, we are taught the ways of life by people at home. Even if we were born in Bandit Gabbar Singh's house or an Honest Police Officer Thakur's home. Our fresh minds are trained in two ways.

Number 1: The house traditions, religion, manners, etc.

Number 2: Society Education and Observation and Life's Experience.

At home, we are strictly told, "This is your surname, and this is our religion, and this is our God." We pray this way to our God. And if you do not follow, then you are mad! Even Our last rites are decided by other humans! That means whatever files have been downloaded to our dear brain's motherboard till now, all those thoughts have been created by some human. Those files are of others: failures, their weaknesses, their wishes, their cowardliness, their bad habits, their bravery, their foolishness, their rivalry, their punishment! Their actions, their ego. Their pride! That is why 'Pathan' thinks he is the best. 'Chauhan' thinks he is the chief. Parents, Siblings, Teachers, Friends, Boyfriends/Girlfriends, Media, Popes, Historians, Education Ministers, Scientists - all humans are just like us.

All the iPhone 16 has the same software, same hardware. All humans have the same software, same hardware just like you. No different types. Wish we 21st-century people had a choice. We all would want to be born in the White House for the money and power. Need to abolish evil from the Earth.

Born Enlighten

All human children are born enlightened. Until 5-6 years, we even manage to stay enlightened.

What is Enlightenment?

Those who can see White is White and Black is Black are all enlightened, very simple. Innocent children are like that only. Those who believe Truth is true and Lies are False are enlightened People. Whenever there is a child growing up in a family, most humans tell their children, this is our family, Our Cast, Our Religion, our Generation; our Actions & Reactions Are the best. We are the one chosen & Loved by God.

Only Us. When an Innocent, enlightened child asks, "And what about the other religious followers?"

Maximum Parents answer, "There are other religions, too, but we are the best."

The child asks again, "What about my good-looking friend in School?"

The answer comes, "Son! The other religion followers are OK-OK, devil types. They will go to Hell!"

The enlightened child does not understand this answer as it is not true! The child is still enlightened in his system; False hasn't been mixed yet. He is not satisfied with the answer. He is confused, and hence, today, most humans are confused! What about the free will given to us by our loving nature? We do not have a clue of free will. We do not miss it at all! We only remember what our elders and Guru taught us.

In our youth, we realise that we were taught in our books to speak the truth! In reality, Presidents/Prime ministers are all lying. Journalists are lying. Judges and lawyers are lying. Family members are lying to each other.

Strange thing is that the liars are also enjoying life! I heard and read that "Telling lies is a sin and those who lie have a snake at home."

Your Journey From Childhood to Being Adult

Everyone is lying, no one is bitten by the snake. In fact, they enjoy supporting lies. Until we reach the corridors of youth, we believe that it's impossible to survive without lying! "Mission Impossible types!" Spend life believing that Lies are Truth, ignoring the Truth. Teenagers get confused and turn Ignorant from Enlightenment! Our life depends on what we input in our mind and body & what we have given out. The following are the emotions which we need to use the least: Anxiety, Confusion, Boredom, Envy, Sadness, Fear & Jealousy. The following emotions need to be used more and more. Adoration, Amusement, Calmness, Excitement, Interest, Joy, Romance, Satisfaction, Sexual desires & Sympathy. Those who can emotionally control themselves, by God's grace, success will be at your feet!

Every human child is born with wisdom. All humans, by birth, are born with wisdom. These so-called gurus, parents, friends, and media train our minds in a manner that they snatch our wisdom from us! In our childhood, they save many files in our minds. Friends and family take away most of the space in our minds. They intentionally/ unintentionally put viruses in our tender minds. They fill up the GBs in our fresh minds with unnecessary details. We do not want any unnecessary files on our mobile/computer, but there are a maximum of useless files in our heads. We let our best computer rust. Our mind-body's 'best system' slowly becomes the 'worst system'.

Are all those humans (gurus) more intelligent than you?

Those who have trained our minds are the files that we carry in our brains regularly. Those whom we follow always, all the time, time after time. To date, our 'Gurus' have trained us if the training of our Gurus is so right and perfect. Why is human suffering so great?

With all due respect to your Gurus! If your Gurus had fed values into your mind and not the virus. If you were taught that we all humans are one and our Creator is also one, then heartily congratulations to you. This world is being sustained because of you and people like you. You and your positivity! Till there is at least one person like you remaining in this world, the world will survive! Wish everyone would follow you, but not everyone is a hero like you. Some of them are villains, too.

Humble & Mentally strong human you are superhuman you are

... AND... The Superhuman Award goes to **YOU.**

Free Will

Nature has given us the power of choice, which means we have free will. We can choose goodness over evil or vice versa. As soon as we are born, we become citizens. We have to be good citizens if we want to choose a hero's character. We have to perform the character of a good human and citizen very well. If you are already doing so, you are successful because you are on the path of truth. Our Creator will always support those humans whose character will have more traits of our nature. The Creator has made this World to prove that truth prevails over evil. He enjoys seeing lies be defeated always. Living naturally, which is very simple & easy, we have to adopt the traits of our nature. Nature would surely take humans to the next level. Those who have nature's characteristics would be enjoying it unimaginably. The choice is yours.

Superhuman. Everything you achieve in this whole life is because of your mind & body, so overhaul it for a healthy-wealthy life.

Character

Hollywood actor "Superhuman" Al Pacino says:

"If you want to be a hero, start living like one."

When God has already created us as superhuman by birth, then why do we need to become anything else? Yes, you can choose your passion, profession, luxury cars, mansions, or private jets—but you will always remain superhuman. How can we become anything else?

One religion believes that to attain human life, a soul has to pass through 80,000 life forms... 80,000 lives, and then finally, this human life!

And yet,

We are wasting it for nothing! alas!!!

The Power of "One"

We always feel, 'What can I do alone?' This is a list of the top ten most influential humans in the world. These individual humans were born alone and have died alone in difficult conditions. There would have been a different world today if all of them were thinking the same!

1. **Name: Muhammad (saw)**

Time Frame: 570–632

Occupation: Secular and religious leaderInfluence: The central human figure of Islam, regarded by Muslims as a Prophet of God and the last messenger. Also active as a social reformer, diplomat, merchant, philosopher, orator, legislator, military leader, humanitarian, and philanthropist.

2. Name: Isaac Newton

Time Frame: 1643–1727

Occupation: Scientist, English physicist, mathematician, astronomer, natural philosopher, alchemist, and theologian. His law of Universal gravitation and three laws of motion laid the groundwork for classical mechanics.

3. Name: Jesus Christ

Time Frame: 7–2 BC – 26–36 AD

Occupation: Spiritual leader The central figure of Christianity, revered by Christians as the Son of God and the incarnation of God, is also regarded as a major prophet in Islam.

4. Name: Buddha

Time Frame: 563–483 BC

Occupation: Spiritual leader, spiritual teacher,and philosopher from ancient India. Founder of Buddhism.

5. Name: Confucius

Time Frame: 551–479 BC

Occupation: Philosopher, Influence: Significant Philosopher, Chinese thinker, and social philosopher, founder of Confucianism whose teachings and philosophy have deeply influenced Chinese, Korean, Japanese, Vietnamese, and Indonesian thought and life.

6. Name: Paul of Tarsus

Time Frame: 5–67 AD

Occupation: Christian apostleOne of the most notable early Christian missionaries, credited with proselytising and spreading Christianity outside of Palestine, mainly to the Romans and author of numerous letters in the New Testament of the Bible.

7. Name: Cai-Lun

Time Frame: 50–121 AD

Occupation: Inventor,Political officials in imperial China were widely regarded as the inventor of paper and the paper-making process.

8. Name: Johannes Gutenberg

Time Frame: 1398–1468

Occupation: Inventor, a German printer who invented the European mechanical printing press.

9. **Name: Christopher Columbus**

Time Frame: 1451–1506

Occupation: ExplorerInfluence: Explorer, Italian navigator, coloniser, and explorer whose voyages led to general European awareness of the American continents.

10. **Name: Albert Einstein**

Time Frame: 1889–1955

Occupation: Physicist Influence: German-born physicist and scientist who developed the special and general theories of relativity and won the Nobel Prize for Physics in 1921 for his explanation of the photoelectric effect. Einstein is generally considered the most influential physicist of the 20th century. Only if one single human wanted to pull the trigger on an atomic bomb could he have destroyed all humans in this world. There is not a single human who has not yet given the order to press the trigger. If Nature/Creator had given any human so much strength that he could destroy or save the universe, then imagine your power. Surely, you are very powerful!

Superhuman Thomas Alva Edison

A single man, Superhuman Thomas Alva Edison, thought, 'I will create a bulb and illuminate the entire world', and he truly lit up the whole planet! He brought light to the darkness of human lives, adding brilliance to all our celebrations! Miracles like this continue to happen in this extraordinary world. We are the Supreme creation of the Almighty. You, too, can do something that benefits humanity.

It's not that none of us among the 96% live a Superhuman life – we all live a Superhuman life to some extent. However, some of us are living at 10%, others at 30%, and a few at 80–90%. Those who live a higher percentage of the superhuman life are utilising more of their superpowers!

Everyone thinks and says, "No one is smarter than me; I am the most intelligent." We all feel that if only the reins of the world were in our hands, we would solve all its problems! But how will we resolve anything without fully utilising our minds? How much can we truly see with a blindfold over our eyes?

When will we be able to use all the power of our brains? Only when we are mentally at peace! Peace—this is the essence of every religion. Peace!

Salute humanity! Humans don't see all the things that are on the Earth and sky, which are all under humans' control. Super strong you are.

Superhuman you are!

Humanity

All humans are One Community!

All Crows in the world are One Community. If a Crow dies, then it is buried with respect by all the Crows and not by pigeons or bears! If any Poacher tries to pick up a baby elephant, then all the elephants will come together to hammer him! Why? Elephant community. At first, all humans were one Community because of Man's ego and differences; they were separated by different colours, different languages, and different cultures. We all humans are One Community! Truth is that Superhuman you are, Superhuman they are, Superhuman we are. All humans are equal. The animals lives shown on the Animal-Planet Channel are all Natural. All those killings are either for survival or defence or to grab a territory. All killings are justified; none are illegitimate killings. Once the Tiger's stomach is full, even if a calf of a deer is close by, he will not touch it. Killing is impossible! What's happening in our world: thousands of people are dying regularly to satisfy the human ego. This means that in today's time, animals are living much better lives than we do, despite 93% of us being hardcore religious and all religions basic concept being social conduct, which means humanity.

The God

God is the truth; He never dies. He was there and will remain forever. God is so great, yet we humans take Him too lightly. But remember, if we remain ignorant despite knowing the truth, punishment is inevitable! What does your God look like?

Our eyes do not have the power to see God... But after this short life test, those who succeed may be able to see God because they will have a new, extraordinary body and enhanced vision. No person or messenger has ever claimed to have seen God. Even messengers themselves are undergoing their life test; they, too, must pass this trial first. He is formless, the source of all energy! He is not human because He created humans. Nowhere in any scripture or from any messenger has it been stated that He looks like a human. He cannot be human! Can a human create the Earth or the sky? We don't even know how many galaxies exist in this universe!

Many believe that God has taken birth in different messengers, but Parmatma (The Supreme God) has no need to come to Earth as a human. Imagine the Creator of this vast universe coming down as a human—eating food, getting tired, sleeping, going to the bathroom, suffering from constipation, and eventually dying!

Could such a being be God?

The Creator is eternal. He doesn't die. He existed, He exists, and He will always exist. God is an immensely vast existence, and we humans take Him too lightly—for which we will undoubtedly face consequences!

Deeds That God Favors (Apart from Prayer)

O' religious ones, if you perform good deeds for yourself and your family, it is worship. If you honestly provide for your family, maintain mental peace, and contribute positively to society, it is worship.

If you feed others, it is an act of devotion. Maintaining cleanliness is worship. Sleeping and waking up on time is righteousness. Protecting yourself and others is worship. Loving animals is worship because love itself is God.

This message is not just for one community; it is for all of humanity. These principles lead to a prosperous life. When all messengers preach the same values, how can any messenger be false? They all taught respect and love.

Think—if all messengers were to meet, would they fight each other, or would they show mutual respect?

Beloved followers of faith, countless other actions are also considered acts of worship.

- Neither the Gita is bad, nor the Quran.
- Neither Hindus are bad, nor Muslims.
- Neither God is bad, nor Bhagwan.
- What is bad is the devil within our minds.

God's Attributes

- He is the Creator and Sustainer.
- He is infinitely merciful.
- He is the most powerful.
- He is the giver of honor.
- He is the ultimate protector.
- He is the forgiver.
- He is the true judge.
- He is gracious and benevolent. God blesses us continuously, and we remain within His blessings eternally because He is our Creator.

God is One

Indeed, our God is one, and we are all part of the same humanity. This is how the system works in our world as well.

There is one head in a family.

One leader in a village.

One leader in a country, whether it is a president or a prime minister.

If there were two heads in a family, village, or country, there would always be conflict and chaos.That's why a single leadership is essential for unity and discipline.We must all understand that our strength lies in our unity.We need to set aside our individual identities and ideologies and accept that we are all part of the same humanity.If all our actions and thoughts are directed toward one common goal—**peace and harmony**—then this world itself becomes a paradise.

If there were multiple gods in the sky, they would be fighting each other, and everything would be destroyed. If we create heaven in our lives, we will receive heaven after this life—if God wills it. But if we make life hell for others, then we will undoubtedly end up in hell. Everything depends on our actions, and deep down, we all know this truth.

Heaven & Hell:

"How is it fair that those who go to heaven will have unlimited wine and women while on Earth intoxication and extramarital relations are considered sins?"

If you pass this test and reach heaven in the afterlife, you will be granted what was forbidden to you here—because your desires remain unfulfilled in this world. Otherwise,

What is the reward for righteousness?

We all know and believe that every action has consequences—whether you sow a thorny bush or a mango tree, you will reap what you sow.

The laws of that world will be different because you would have already passed the test.

Does God lack resources?

Even on this Earth, God has provided everything in abundance, but it is humans who have created rationing and scarcity. Every place has its own constitution. For example:

- If you consume marijuana in India, you might get arrested.
- But in America, it's not an issue.

Similarly, life on Earth is a test that requires self-control. And why is self-control needed?

Because humans have been given enormous power, far beyond our comprehension. Just one person pressing a nuclear bomb button can turn the entire world into a fireball. That is how much power a single human being holds!

The Traits of Satan

- Liar
- Deceiver
- Vengeful
- Cunning
- Hypocritical
- Cruel
- Opponent of God's rule

Satan exists within our hearts. He is a conceptual character created by God to test us in this life examination. But God has also given us the power to choose... Free Will. Now, we can either enlarge the idea of Satan in our minds, turn him into a ghost, and keep fearing him... Or we can live a fearless life— Superhuman life, Enjoying every moment until our last breath! Because—

"The path of God is the simplest path."

Stay Enlightened

Just as we were born with wisdom, we must remain so. We can take good lessons from our Gurus and elders, but now you must take control of your own life. It's not necessary that everything elders say is correct – if it were, there would be peace in the world. Often, corrupt politicians ruin the future of an entire nation's youth.

In God's live movie, you are the hero or heroine. If you are mentally healthy, enjoy the life of a Superhuman. You are a star, you are a celebrity, so celebrate your beautiful life. You know this journey of life is a mind game, and you must win it. Peace is where true power lies—that is the essence of every religion. People think staying calm is the hardest thing to do, but that's not true. We spend most of the day pointing out others' mistakes.

You might say, "How can one remain calm in traffic or a crowd? How can one stay calm in financial struggles?"

This is all just talk. But have you noticed how often people get upset in crowds or traffic? They say, "It's So crowded!" or in traffic, "There's so much traffic!" And what about us?

We are the traffic. We are the crowd! It's all a MIND GAME.

"Enlighten your mind to be aware of your own superpowers." (Superhuman Django)

Success

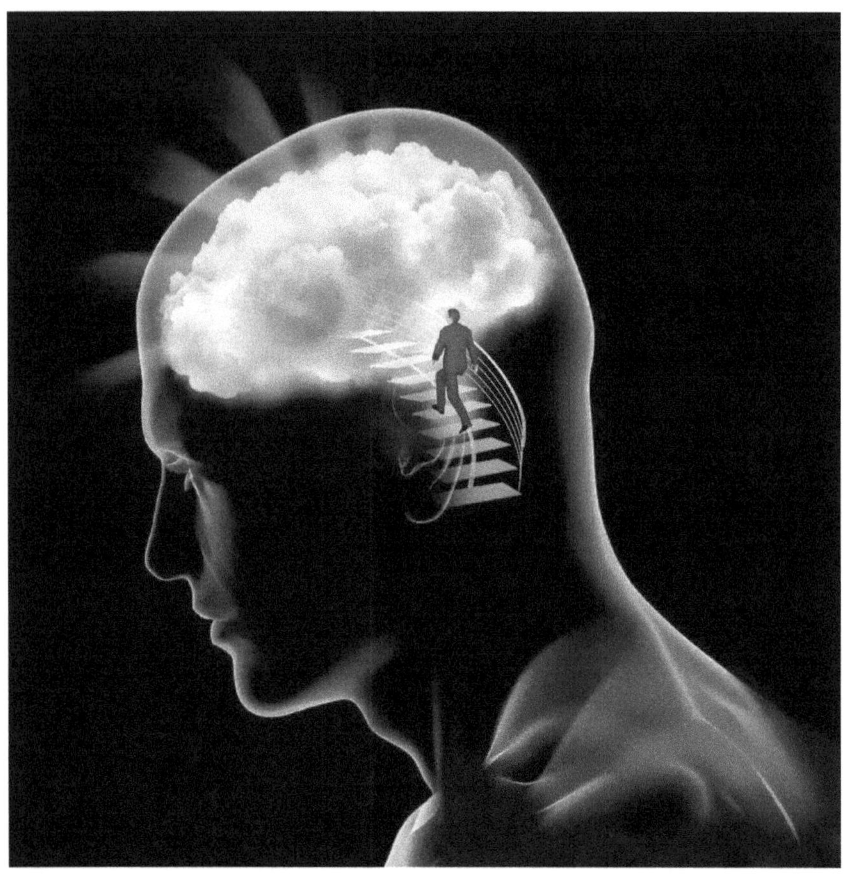

... Keep your mind's light on to use your superpowers... Superhuman Django

The mind is the motherboard of the body. Just as an electrical system runs a machine, your mind operates like a device. Just as you keep only useful apps on your mobile or computer and remove the unnecessary ones, you should do the same with your mind's motherboard—store only essential thoughts to live a natural and peaceful life.Stop living in the past. That time is gone. There is no benefit in regretting the past, but you can surely learn from it. Just as we format our mobile or laptop, we must also format our minds. For the happiness of your mind, format it now! Your mind is your servant, so the control should be in your hands, not the other way around. Remember, in the end, it's only you who has to take responsibility—no one else!If we understand even a little about our car's engine, it benefits us throughout our lives. That is why understanding our mind and body is the most important thing.

Free Your Mind from Negativity:

Start each day by reviewing your daily schedule. From waking up to going to bed, observe your routine and treat everyone you meet as a superhuman. While it's natural to consider yourself superior, understand that others have the same right to feel the same about themselves. Just as you keep only useful apps on your mobile or computer and delete the rest, do the same with your mind's motherboard. Retain onlyWhat is useful?

Regularly 'format' your mind, just like formatting a mobile or laptop. If you intrude into someone else's universe, it will bring unrest, and if someone enters your universe, they will regret it. Protect yourself from mental and physical abuse.

The body and soul are like a tyre and tube—your body is the tyre, and you, the soul, are the tube within. Happiness depends on providing the right amount of oxygen to your mind and body. In emergencies, hospitals prioritise oxygen because the lack of it can destroy vital organs or even lead to death. After over 40 years of trying countless exercises, I've found most of them are painful, which is why people avoid them. However, I discovered exercises that are enjoyable and keep me fit, almost like playing a game. So far is because of your body and mind, and whatever you achieve in the future will also depend on them. Start using your superpowers right now.

The Superhuman Formula: Apply the Superhuman Formula to lead a healthy and wealthy life. Wake up to this realisation now—because whenever you awaken, it's the dawn of a new day!

Double Mind

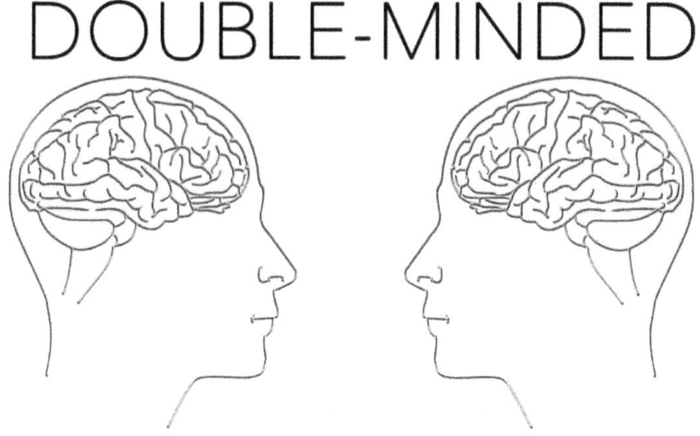

Nature has given us innumerous Superpowers. If we remain double-minded about our future, we are unable to harness those powers. Those who work towards their goals with a single-minded focus become scientists, doctors, engineers, pilots, and businessmen. Whatever you want to become, first think about it completely, feel it, and dedicate yourself to it.

"If one person says he can and another says he cannot, then often both are right."

(Superhuman Will Smith.)

The Mechanism of Your Mind & Body

Understanding Your Mind and Body

If we understand even a little about how our car engine works, we benefit from it for a lifetime. That is why understanding our mind and body is the most important thing.

Please note: You don't have a soul; you are the soul. For example, when I die, I will be gone. After death, my body will be considered lifeless. My mind and body are my servants, so why not use them as tools? If you don't misuse your mind and body, you will experience heaven right here on Earth!

Your Body is a Gadget: Your body is a gadget, just like your mobile phone or computer. Every gadget is your servant, and your body is no different. Take care of your body just like you care for your devices—in fact, even more.

Everything you have achieved so far has been possible because of your mind and body. They are the most advanced machines you will ever own. Some people buy expensive, high-tech gadgets but never use their full potential. Similarly, most of us fail to use the full potential of our minds and bodies.

Discover Your Body's Superpowers: Only 4% of people deeply understand their mind and body, and they are the ones who lead the rest. So why not become one of those shining stars? By understanding your physical system, you can live a healthy and prosperous life.

Think of Iron Man's suit: the suit is external, but Tony Stark is inside, controlling it. Likewise, your body is your suit, and you are the soul within it. Your body is temporary and typically lasts 100 to 150 years, but eventually, it will wear out. However, if you care for it properly, you can delay that decline. Just like Parsis maintain their cars so well that even old ones sell for a higher price, you can maintain your body for better performance.

Cleaning the Mind: Stop living in the past; it's already gone. Imagine I have only ten days left to live, but I spend those ten days dwelling on sad memories from the past. When the tenth day comes and I die, I would have already been dead inside due to those burdensome thoughts.

So, there's no point regretting the past; learn from it instead. Just like you format your phone or computer when it gets overloaded, you need to format your mind as well. For the sake of your happiness—format it right now!Your mind is your servant; you need to control it, not let it control you.

Remember: Until your last breath, you are responsible for yourself and your family —no one else.

So, take charge of your life right now; sit in the driver's seat of your life's journey. It's your life, and only you can drive and repair (heal) its vehicle. Your dreams will come true with the help of your mind and body. If you stay mentally healthy, you will stay physically healthy—and a healthy person is more likely to succeed in accumulating wealth.

Start using your superpowers from today!

Illness

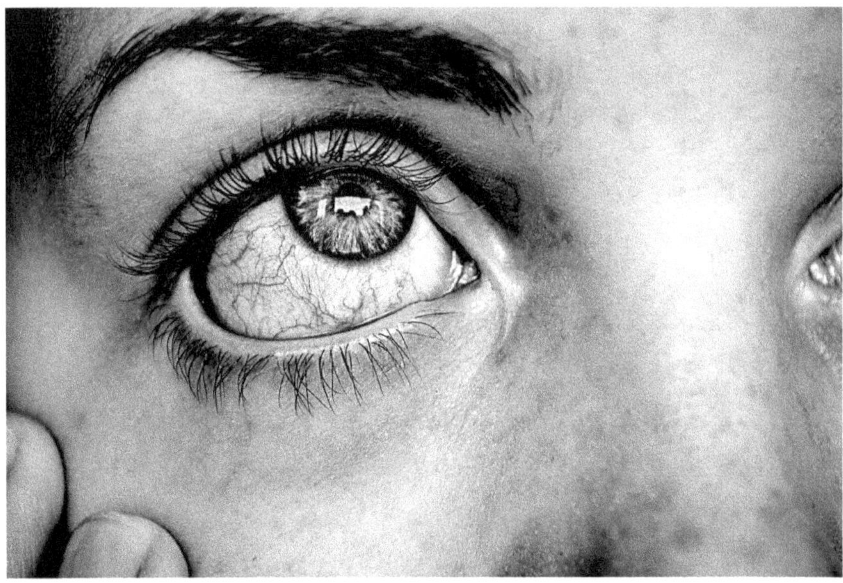

The main cause of maximum diseases is mind & body abuse. If a person lives a virus free life then disease won't even get close. A person who doesn't abuse mind & body then his life would be healthy and wealthy surely.

Emotional Power

We are all, in a way, like robots, but we believe that robots are stronger than us because they are made of metal. However, humans can melt metal with ease.

Our greatest strength is that we are emotional beings. Our bodies hold emotions that make us alive and unique. Science is now trying to instill emotions in robots, but the irony is that we humans fail to understand the true power of our emotions. Not only do we fail to comprehend them, but we also waste them unnecessarily.

The biggest problem is that we do not use our emotions in the right place. We treat emotions as "free commodities" and spend them carelessly.

- We start hating others for no reason.
- Anger and irritation are always ready within us.

- Fear weakens us unnecessarily.
- We waste our entire lives worrying about the future.
- We become anxious thinking about what others are doing.
- We get overly invested in a celebrity's watch, house, or life, draining our emotions on meaningless things.
- If a friend progresses more than us, we develop feelings of inferiority or jealousy.

The Power of Emotions

Emotions are our greatest strength. If we learn to control our emotions, we can make our lives completely successful. This power gives us the ability to change instantly.

- If you are doing well, you can make it even better.
- If you are on the wrong path, you can immediately correct yourself and move in the right direction.

Emotional Awareness

Each of us has an emotional awareness within us.

- This awareness teaches us to differentiate between good and bad.
- It makes us realize whether what we are doing is right or wrong.
- Within us, there is a scale of emotions that helps us understand which direction we should take.
- This scale gives us a sense of right and wrong, and this very awareness makes us better human beings.

Emotions are our greatest asset. Learn to use them wisely. Do not waste your emotions by imitating others, feeling jealous, or worrying unnecessarily.

Channel your emotions in the right direction.

Use your power of choice and strive to improve yourself.

To succeed in every test of life, maintain the right balance between your emotions and actions. Remember, emotional awareness is the true essence of life. Understand it, embrace it, and steer your life in the right direction.

If we can control our emotions, life will be successful. Apart from superpowers, we also have an incredible power—the power of choice. By using this power,l. You can even save someone's life or take someone's life. You can prevent a rape from happening, or you can commit rape. This is proof that this life is our test. Inside you is emotional awareness, which allows you to distinguish between good and bad.

You can also feel whether you are doing something right or wrong because you have a balance of emotions within you.

Your small world sees you healthy and happy, they will be inspired to bring positive changes in their own lives. This chain reaction can fill the entire world with positivity.

Your Small World

In everyone's life, there are only 10-20 people who are extremely important. Out of These 8-10 are in our inner circle with whom we meet every day. The outer world consists of co-workers, travellers, etc.

The 5-7 closest people are our small world. You and your family and friends—now you know that all of them are superhumans, just like you. We need to understand that everyone is playing their role in this live movie—some doing good, some doing bad. It's just like when we are sitting in an exam hall; we focus on our own paper and not on other papers. This life is a test, but in this test, we often do the opposite. Instead of focusing on ourselves, we turn into examiners for everyone else. Some may follow your thoughts, and some may oppose them! Our life often gets wasted in criticising others. We are often troubled thinking, "My husband/wife isn't good; my boss isn't good; my relatives are terrible; my friends are my enemies; this world is bad." We are constantly concerned with correcting others, whereas the truth is that no one has ever been able to change someone else. Do you think you can change your husband/wife? Your spouse wants to change you!

Superhuman Tolstoy said, **"Everyone wants to change the world, but no one is ready to change themselves."**

Life begins to improve as soon as we realise that we need to work on ourselves, BUT not on others. We need to cleanse our own minds. As you work on yourself, you will become more elevated, healthy, and wealthy! After 40 days, you will see that the people around you will begin to follow you, and with your positivity, those who were close to you will become even closer, while those you wanted to distance from your life will naturally fade away.

Daily Routine (24x7)

From the moment we wake up to when we return to bed, our day follows a cycle. We need to evaluate our schedule and perceive everyone we meet as superhumans.

Dependency on Medications After 40:

After turning 40, most people rely on medicines, sometimes keeping multiple pillboxes. Pharmacy stores open 24/7 are increasing, even though more than half of the diseases stem from our thoughts. We can heal ourselves like superheroes.

Healthy

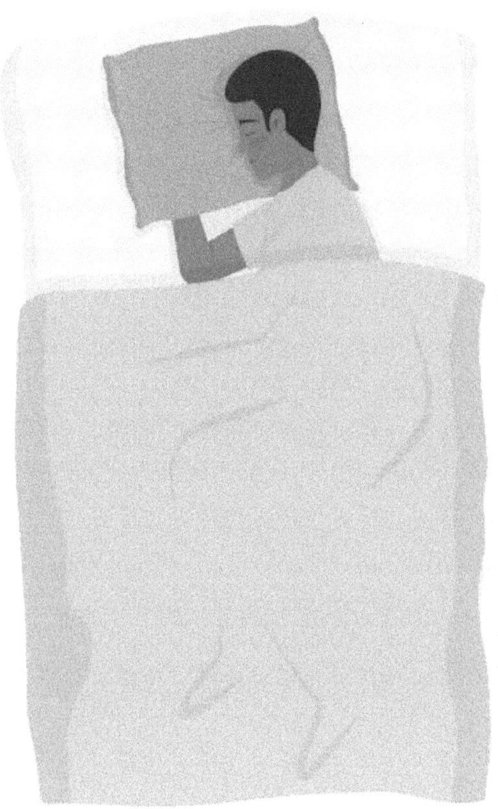

Applying Dr. & Master Sha's technique and Superhuman Wim Hof's breathing technique, we can easily heal ourselves.

I have the power to heal myself; you have the power to heal yourself; let's heal the world...

Superhuman Dr.& Master Sha After following Master Sha and Superhuman Wim Hof techniques, I have cured myself of diseases like Varicose veins, High BP, Slip disc, Chronic Acidity, Arthritis, Cyst in the left kidney & many more. After seeing positive results for myself, I started teaching patients to self-heal themselves, and many patients have recovered. Cancer patient Kusum Jain has cured herself of cancer, and now she is cancer-free.

10 Years ago, I spread this concept in my circle, which resulted in a 'Superhuman

Society'. This 'Superhuman you are' formula is where we believe and practice that we all are as important as we are. I shared this thought with 100 humans who applied it to themselves. Everyone saw and felt that their lives had become healthy and wealthy. They are living a cool & calm life today. Their mind is virus-free, and if you are mentally healthy, then it becomes easy to earn more wealth. You may want to earn in lakhs today, but if you mentally improve your health, you will earn in Crores. **The Superhuman formula is really simply superb.**

Superhuman Wim Hof 'The Iceman'

Superhuman Wim Hof, the "IceMan"enjoys a bath in freezing minus 40-degree temperature, which is a world record. Any normal human being would freeze to death in these temperatures.

Wim Hof breathing exercise:.

We restore enough oxygen in our minds and bodies.

The main cause of most diseases is that oxygen does not reach those body parts. Every day, when we fill the oxygen tank in the first place, we will be mentally healthy for 24 hours. If we are mentally healthy, we are physically healthy too. If we stay mentally and physically healthy, then we can easily be wealthy because whatever we achieve, we achieve through our mind and body only.

You will be happy when your brain and physical body receive the right amount of oxygen. In emergency situations, patients are given oxygen in the hospital ICU first. If the oxygen supply is less, our vital organs get damaged, and humans die without oxygen.

I have been exercising for the last 30 years; I have tried many different exercises in my lifetime. Almost all exercises are strenuous; hence, humans do not like to exercise, even though I have had the opportunity to do non-strenuous exercises in this journey of life. The best exercises that I have experienced are the **"Superhuman exercises"**.

A 2-year-old child to a 150-year-old person can do these exercises with a smile. I strongly recommend Superhuman Wim Hof's breathing technique. This is the world's best exercise, which you can do even while lying on your bed. Superhuman Wim Hof has also created a world record for walking in the desert at over 50 degrees Celsius without water. Superhuman Wim Hof has taught us that we can control our own body temperature just like how air conditioners operate. Believe me, due to this breathing exercise, you will be able to control your body temperature. My body power has increased to the next level. Many Hollywood personalities are learning from wim hof's breathing technique and I am spreading this in bollywood.

Today I feel 5-7 degrees Celsius lower in the hot weather and the same in winter.

Superhuman Non-Strenuous Exercises

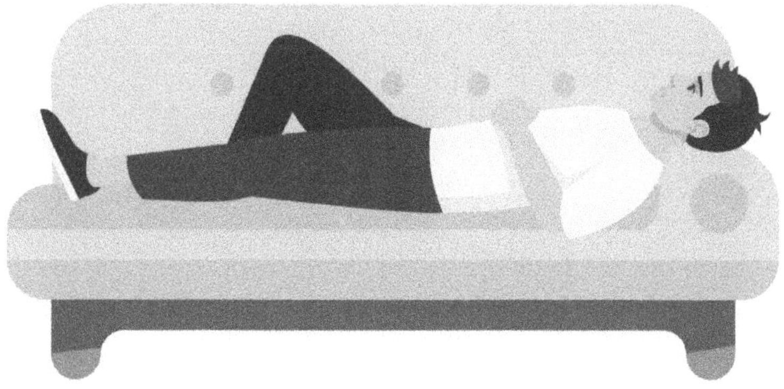

Stretching:

Animals do not exercise, but they do stretching, and they are super fit. You, too, can also do stretching. You can stretch while sitting, standing, or lying on the bed.3. Avoid body abuse. It's a saying that "We are what we eat." It's really true. When we smoke, we never think it might give us cancer, but we are sure it's not going to happen. Lakhs of humans get cancer because of smoking. When we abuse our body, we think it's not going to affect us, but later on, when we get sick, we admit it's happening because of our body abuse.

Avoid Emotional Abuse:

To be emotionally abused means to abuse our soul. We have limited energy in 24 hours. Do we waste our energy listening to gossip or gossiping? Do we waste it in fear? Do we burn it in hatred? We have free will. We have our minds and our moments of life. If we bring peace to our souls, then automatically, we are successful. Politics and religion are both respectful and important subjects. Avoid political and religious confrontations; with confrontations, there are no gains. Instead of debating on religion, it is better to apply it practically! From your social conduct only, it is clear that our religion is good or We are just a pretender. Differences in political views also cause animosity between humans.

Instead of arguing, it's better to go and vote for your favourite party on Election Day.

Meditation: this is the best exercise to focus your mind towards your goal.all the messengers and scientists and great achievers have one thing in common that they all used to meditate.

Wealthy

Superhuman Bill Gates Said... **If you are born in a poor household, it's not your fault, but if you die in a poor household, then it's your fault!**

We all want to earn a lot of money so that we can buy the world's best properties, cars, jewelry, and savings. This is a great thing! If you want to achieve even more, that's good news. It is human nature to always want more, and that's exactly why we have reached the moon!

Only 4% of the world's population lives a superhuman life, and these are the same 4% who are the wealthiest people on the planet. For them, buying a private jet or an island is no big deal. They run the world on their own terms and have proven that **Money is power:**

Today, we see that only the wealthy are powerful. We all work hard to earn money. Honest people earn money through honesty, while some are willing to do anything to get rich. Some people only think about "money, money, money," but just thinking about it doesn't bring wealth. Money is a productive result of your work. If you work, you will earn money. This is a science. Just like planting seeds leads to fruits, hard work leads to rewards. But humans want money quickly—overnight, instantly—because we are impatient. All successful people say: Have patience! "Keep planting seeds, and you will have a blooming garden."

It's possible that the person or company for whom you worked honestly for years may give you nothing in return or may have already done so. But the universe follows a Science—your hard work is already recorded; it has not gone to waste. Stay faithful to God, and one day, an unexpected messenger will bring you news beyond your imagination—news that may change your life for the better!

That's why it is said:

"Allah is the Most Merciful and Compassionate." "Ishwar-Allah, Your Names Are One; O Lord, Grant Everyone Wisdom!"

Superhuman Bruce Lipton

Says: "**The human mind is extremely powerful.**" **Humans can explore, invent, experience, and even destroy through their thoughts.**

Bruce Lipton dedicated 35 years of his life to NASA and proved that under special circumstances, every human uses 100% of their brain power. For example, if a person saves a drowning child from a flowing river, they are not just using 5-6% of their brain but 100%.

Some people live a superhuman life by making the right use of their minds even in normal circumstances. These people live in the present moment—neither lost in the past nor worried about the future.

Many people who have achieved everything in life still live in deep sadness. Cars have been invented, airplanes have been built, mobile phones and the internet have revolutionized the world. Spacecraft, flying suits, rockets, submarines, and Segways have been created. Humans have reshaped the universe over and over again, giving everything a new direction. But one question still remains—when will we truly enjoy life?

Are we waiting for a grand X-Mas?

- Whenever we are bathing, our mind is somewhere else.
- Whenever we are eating, our thoughts are tangled in something else.
- Even during romance, our attention is drifting elsewhere.

Reincarnation & Bruce Lipton's Spiritual View

There are many interesting similarities in spiritual perspectives on reincarnation.

Bruce Liptonbelief: The soul is something separate is incorrect. He explains that the soul is energy, and energy can never be destroyed; it only transfers. At 76 years old, Bruce Lipton appears enthusiastic and joyful in his recent videos. He shared that he and his wife are now **free from the fear of death.**

Judgement Day

Those who believe that we will not rise again must consider that one cannot simply disappear from the universe. Where and how can we be thrown out of the universe? God will certainly recreate you. According to religious beliefs, on the Day of Judgment, all humans will rise from the earth with new bodies, much like the character Sandman from the movie "Spider-Man." On that day, our deeds will be accounted for because, while justice is absent in this world, there must be a place where nature ensures justice. Every individual will receive their report card, and even the smallest deeds—good or bad—will be presented before them.

This body is mortal, but the next body will be eternal. If someone doubts that we will not rise again, they should remember that we were once nothing. Just as nature created us the first time, why would it be difficult to recreate us again? If someone can make something once, making it again is even easier. Like barren land that comes to life after rain, humans too will rise again. All religions state that once eternal life begins, death will no longer exist.

Rebirth is not merely a spiritual belief; it is scientifically plausible as well. Humans should focus on improving their deeds and thoughts. As you sow, so shall you reap. If this life resembles heaven, the next will too. If this life is like hell, the next will mirror it because experiences shape outcomes. Just as one trusts a doctor with an injection rather than an unqualified person, similarly, after passing this life-test, one will enjoy eternal bliss, as humans are God's finest creation.

Controlling Desires: We must not follow all our desires, as they lead us astray from the path of truth. Those who avoid major sins will be forgiven by God. No person will bear another's burden. Those who present themselves before God with a pure heart—like the one given to them at birth—will succeed. Believers trust in the rewards of paradise.

In heaven, time will not exist, similar to a black hole. Whether a person dies young or old, they will be resurrected young and remain so forever. Strength is required to endure punishment or enjoy pleasures.

Some religious individuals believe they will become angels in the next life. But if asked, most would want to retain their current appearance, not transform into angels. Our Creator understands our desires far better than we can imagine.

The wrongdoers will face hardship, proving the victory of truth over falsehood, which pleases God because truth is God.

In heaven, there will always be a celebration because those who followed God's path will be His guests. Imagine being a guest of God!

Even in this life, we wish to party endlessly, but responsibilities and societal constraints prevent us. Heaven's constitution will be different—eternal joy without concerns.

As the saying goes: "As you sow, so shall you reap—disbelieve it and test it. Heaven and hell exist—die and see it."

Format Your Mind Now!

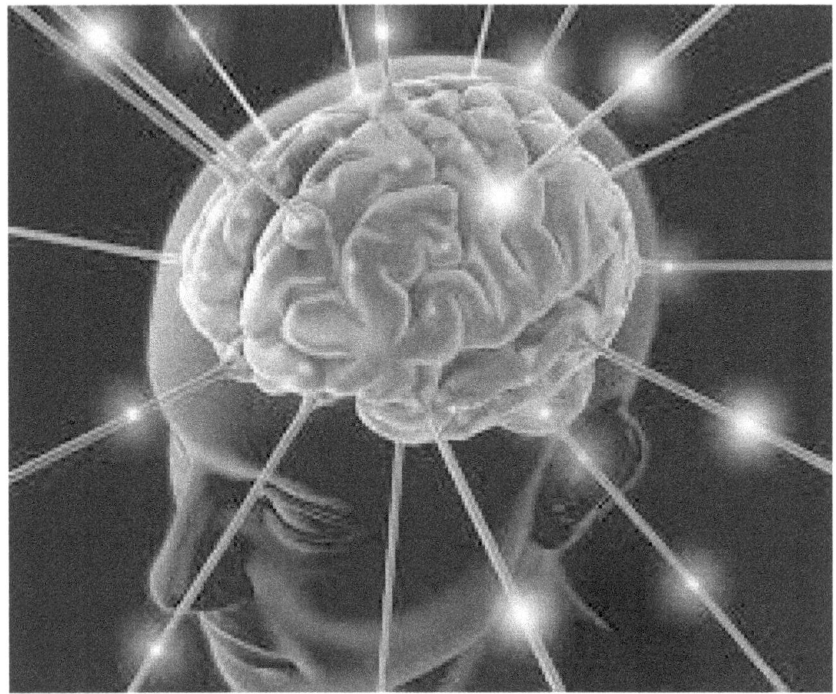

Format your mind instantly!

Politics and Religion: Both are esteemed and important subjects. Your social behavior should reflect your religion. Political differences also create distances between people. Instead of debating, vote for your favorite party on election day.

Has anyone ever won in the debate of religion and politics?

Or will anyone ever win?

Today, most people are ruining their lives based on politics and religion. Just think, the person who will become the Prime Minister is also just a human like you.

Why should we follow **their agenda?**

Why not create **our own agenda** where people work for THEMSELVES?

We are so caught up in the media, main news, and television drama, that our first concern upon waking up and going to bed is whether our preferred party won and whether our rival party lost. Were we born for others?

The day I stopped debating religion and politics, I suddenly had more energy. This energy can now be used to make bigger plans.

Try this method, it's very important. You should adopt it with determination and enjoy the benefits!

We have free will, our own mind, and moments of life.

If we bring peace to our minds, we become successful right away. Without peace, there is no success. Ask any rich person why they don't sleep well at night.

Why do famous and wealthy people commit suicide?

If you have peace, you are successful every moment. If I die peacefully, my loved ones will pray for my soul. Otherwise, why do we, on social media, say "RIP" after someone's death?

We wish we had given them peace while they were alive, then we would have received peace (success) ourselves. What we sow, we reap.

If we experience heaven here, we will experience it there too. It all depends on our experiences, as you know. Hell is harder to achieve. By igniting various desires and a burning wish to destroy others, we ourselves will eventually vanish. But the bad air left behind will be required in hell forever, while those who provide and receive peace will be guests of God.

Free will and our actions today will define our tomorrow. Everything depends on our deeds, and it's all about experiences.

Take control of your life **from now onwards** because it's **your life superhuman!!!**

The End

Superhuman Azimji Premji

Superhuman Azimji Premji says: **"If people are not mocking your goal, then your goal is too small."**

That's why my goal is very big, and it's for the world to adopt the Superhuman Society, where We respect one another and consider others as Superhumans, raising the banner of humanity.

Because you are Superhuman, they are Superhuman, and we all are Superhuman.

Your Superhuman Society

Superhuman Society: The vision and core mantra of the Superhuman Society is based on the idea that every individual should be seen as a "Superhuman." The aim is to unite all of humanity, where we respect each other and treat everyone equally as Superhumans. This book is an effort to promote this idea. I have created a list to reflect the acceptance and importance of this idea. The people included in this list come from various religions, professions, and backgrounds. To promote this idea, a dedicated team of 100 members has supported me unconditionally. I sincerely thank all these Superhumans because they are the foundation of this society.

When I shared this idea with Superhuman Anil Senior, he accepted it positively and provided full support. Anil assisted me in my research process and helped me learn about Superhuman Wim Hof and motivational speaker Tony Robbins. Superhuman Anil has always encouraged me. Completing this book would not have been possible without him and the "Superhuman Passionate Hundred Team.

Values of the Superhuman Society:

- Superhumans are peacebuilders.
- Superhumans learn from the past, live in the present, and design their future.
- Superhumans love their homeland.
- Superhumans maintain a balanced physical energy.
- Superhumans work on themselves instead of criticizing others.
- Superhumans inspire others with positive energy.
- Superhumans believe that every human is a complete universe in themselves.
- Superhumans manage their time and respect others' time.
- Superhumans believe that life is the greatest gift from God.
- Superhumans don't believe in limitations.
- Superhumans don't wait for magic because humans create their own magic, thus They live a miraculous life.
- Superhumans consider gratitude as their only perspective and are free from ego.

Superhuman Passionate 100 Team

The List of names from various professions such as Actors, Directors, Politicians, Businessmen & Service men etc.

Anil Senior - Film Director, Mohammad Aslam - Actor, Shivam Agarwal - Actor, Parvez Alam - Writer/Director, Nikita Dixit - Actress, Gautam Dutta - Director, Mamta Nigam - Actress, Ramesh Kumar - Businessman, Sharif Khan - Politician, Akbar Naqvi - Producer/Businessman, Abeer Khan - Journalist, Shivam Makan - Cameraman, Rashmi Singh - Ayurvedic Doctor, E. Nivas - Director, Amit Kumar - CBI Officer, Salim Hussain - Businessman, Anas Khan - Producer/Actor, Haji Shakeel Qureshi - Businessman, Shadab Khan - Director, Sikandar Mirza - Producer, Pooja Saxena - Actress, Zia Siddiqui - Actress, Munawwar Khan - Athlete (Shooting), Waqar Sheikh - Shipping Business, Aniket - Restaurant Businessman, Komal Yadav - Actress, Rizwan Sikandar - Actor, Prince Paul - Restaurant Businessman, Arfan Khan - Actor,

Prerna Trivedi - Actress, Abhinav Dixit - Actor, Fazal Khan - Student, Jehan Khan - Student, Roshan Khan - Teacher, Nafisa Ali - Politician, Imtiaz Sheikh - Businessman, Muskan Seth - Executive Producer, Roshni Singh - Actress, Sana Khan - Actress, Kalpana Kumar - Actress, Satish Kumar - Businessman, Shadab Siddiqui - Director, Manish Jha - Director, Anand Shetty - Action Director, Devroon Day - Actor, Firoz Sheikh - Social Worker, Ejaz Khan - Actor, Trilok Karnwanshi - Actor, Rohit Negi - Businessman, Gulshan Chauhan - Actor, Anil Thakur - Super Cop, Firoz Khan - Actor, Sunita Bajaj - Executive Producer, Rehan Khan - Boxer/Actor, Mehboob Khan - Interior Designer, Veena Jain - Actress, Raiya Labib - Model, Shazia Jafri - Designer, Shakeel Akhtar - Cinematographer, Pradeep Singh - Actor, Shabahat Mujtaba - Web Developer, Sajida Khan - Actress, Arif Lashkaria - Politician, Asad Lashkaria - Politician, Shweta Singh - Homemaker, Shamim Ahmed Gubreta - Businessman, Ram Choyal - Director, Akshay Shukla - Theater Director, Yogesh Yogi - Actor, Sunil Bhargav - Actor, Priya Vishwanath - Actor, Afroz Babar - Car Dealer, Noor Siddiqui - Director, Nawab Shah - Actor, Ali Sheikh - Stuntman, Sachin Adavanshi (CEO of FFW), Amar - Businessman, Arafat Mahmood - Lyricist, Mohammad Anwar - Businessman, Surendra Sagar - Actor, Bhojraj - Actor, Mohammad Sultan - Businessman, Rabia Sultan - Homemaker, Zafar Khan - Businessman, Firdaus Khan - Actress, Surendra Sharma - Manager, Jigyasa Yaduvanshi - Actress, Jaiveer - Director/Distributor, Mandhir Singh - Radio Channel Owner, Asima Bhatt - Actress, Aslam Khan - Car Mechanic, Nazim Khan - Advocate, Naseem Sami - Businessman, Ejaz Ahmed - Businessman, Zeenat - Homemaker, Sonia Qureshi - Service Sector, Firdaus Maroof - Teacher, Prashant Patil - IAS Officer, Rocky Roshan - Film Director/Writer, Rajpal Yadav - Actor.

This list represents a small India in itself.

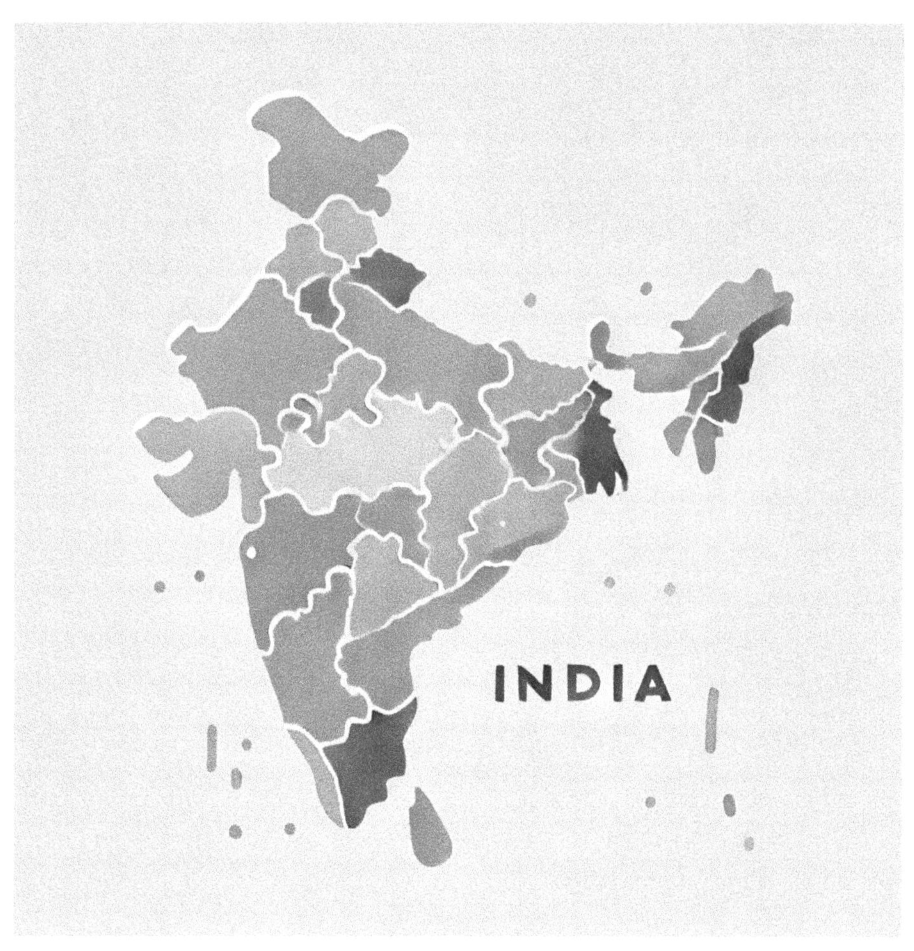

Jay Hind

Become a part of the Superhuman Society and unite your world because... **You are, a born SUPERHUMAN.**

www.superhumanur.com
superhumanfoundation@gmail.com
mobile:9821786321